101 *Youth Soccer* Drills

Age 12 to 16

Also available from Reedswain Inc.

101 Youth Soccer Drills
Age 7 to 11
Malcolm Cook
ISBN # 1-890946-22-2

Soccer Training Drills – 6th Edition
Games, Drills and Fitness Practices
Malcolm Cook and Nick Whitehead
ISBN # 1-890946-20-6

101 *Youth Soccer* Drills

Malcolm Cook

Reedswain Inc. • Spring City, PA

This edition published in 1999 in the United States by
Reedswain Inc., 612 Pughtown Road, Spring City, PA 19475

Published by special arrangement with
A & C Black (Publishers) Ltd
35 Bedford Row, London WC1R 4JH

International Standard Book Number: 1-890946-23-0
Library of Congress Catalog Card Number: 99-070332

Acknowledgements
Cover photographs courtesy of Action Images Plc.
Textual photographs courtesy of Allsport UK Ltd.
Illustrations on pages 11–13 by Jean Ashley.
All other illustrations by Sue Dods.

Printed in Great Britain

REEDSWAIN VIDEOS AND BOOKS, INC.
612 Pughtown Road • Spring City, Pennsylvania 19475
1-800-331-5191
www.reedswain.com

CONTENTS

ACKNOWLEDGEMENTS

There are several people who I would like to thank for their help in the production of this book. First, my valued friend Christine Holmes for her kindness and sheer professionalism in proofreading and typing the script, all within the deadline – I could not have done it without her. Second, thanks also to Cheryl Rose at A & C Black for her continual support. Last, but not least, thanks to Dario Gradi (Manager, Crewe Alexandra Football Club), one of the best coaches of young players in international football, for honouring this book with his Foreword. Finally, best wishes to all the coaches who work with young players, wherever you are – your work makes a difference and is vitally important to the future of our great game. Good coaching!

FOREWORD

Malcolm and I first met in the late 1960s, just as we were both making the transition from players to coaches. I became the Football Association's first regional coach for London with responsibility for setting up coaching demonstrations and general training for coaches; Malcolm had started coaching schoolboys and young professional players.

Malcolm was an enthusiastic searcher of coaching knowledge in those days and this book shows that he has discovered a sound system of practice drills for coaches to use with youngsters who are learning the game. Coaches, particularly those who have been working with the same group of players for more than a season, are always looking for the best drills that can be applied easily on the field, fresh moves to introduce to the game plan or ways to stimulate the old tried-and-tested drills.

101 Youth Soccer Drills is an essential reference on practical drills for coaches, who can benefit from Malcolm's years of experience and coaching of young soccer players.

Dario Gradi
Manager
Crewe Alexandra Football Club

Arthur Numan, the Dutch left-sided defender, shows a good balance in his defensive and attacking functions. He is a tenacious opponent who will wait for the opportune moment to tackle quickly for the ball. On the attack he uses his excellent left foot to curl crosses into the penalty box or to sweetly strike the ball towards goal. *Photo: Alex Livesey*

INTRODUCTION

This book has been written to help coaches, teachers and parents to maximise the results of their practice sessions with young footballers. The main aim of the book is to provide a detailed programme of specific, progressive and realistic drills for young players, which, if used regularly, will systematically improve their playing skills. The emphasis is on drills that are geared to the specific needs of youngsters between the ages of 12 and 16.

As young players become adolescents they can start to learn more advanced technical skills and how to use these skills in realistic, game-like situations. During adolescence, youngsters become more competitive, especially the more mature players, and this needs to be channelled correctly for their performance to accelerate in the optimum way. Coaches, teachers and parents should ensure that youngsters at this age are not treated like 'mini-adults' in practice sessions. They need to be supported, inspired and guided to ensure that each one of them can fully maximise their playing potential.

My hope is that this book will become an essential resource of functional drills for coaches, teachers and parents who want their young players to become the best that they can be.

Although the word 'he' is used throughout the book, this is only for convenience and should be taken to mean 'he' or 'she' to recognise that female players continue to give much to the sport and are continuing to develop in their own right.

KEY TO DIAGRAMS

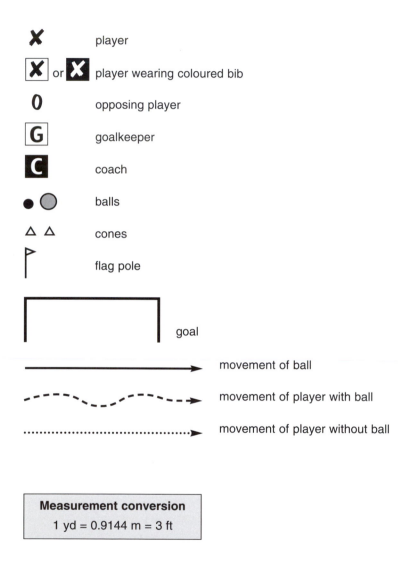

X   player

X or **X**   player wearing coloured bib

0   opposing player

G   goalkeeper

C   coach

● ○   balls

△ △   cones

⚑   flag pole

                          goal

———————▶   movement of ball

– – – – –▶   movement of player with ball

· · · · · · · ·▶   movement of player without ball

Measurement conversion
1 yd = 0.9144 m = 3 ft

Notes
• The cones, which are used for markers, are not always mentioned in the practice set-up for the drill, but they are listed in the equipment.
• Any other suitable piece of equipment can be used to substitute for the cones and flag poles.

Chapter 1

PRACTICE ORGANISATION

The good coach will endeavour to produce an effective learning environment for his players that promotes safety, fun, purpose and ensures progression. He should plan each session beforehand and decide on the skills or topics that he wishes his players to learn. He can select the combinations of drills from the book that he will use in his session and should arrive early at practice in order to set up and prepare equipment for the players. Good organisation generally makes for good coaching and motivation. Here are some basic guidelines for the coach to consider when using the drills from this book.

PRACTICE SERVICE

The coach will have to demonstrate and allow his players to practise ways of serving the ball to their team-mates. Some of the techniques will be familiar to them while some will be relatively new; however, all of them will be valuable for their training. The majority of service actions are by hand as this tends to guarantee accuracy. However, as soon as the player can consistently kick the ball well he can serve in this manner too.

These are the service techniques:

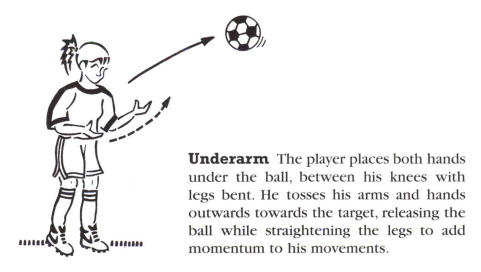

Underarm The player places both hands under the ball, between his knees with legs bent. He tosses his arms and hands outwards towards the target, releasing the ball while straightening the legs to add momentum to his movements.

Throw-in The player places both hands around the back of the ball, which rests on the back of his neck. With one leg in front of the other to give himself a more balanced position, he bends his upper body backwards before swinging forwards in a smooth motion to thrust the arms forwards and send the ball on its way.

Javelin The player balances the ball using one hand and wrist to secure it. The body is turned side-on with the other arm aimed towards the intended target. The player then whips his arm over and through to hurl the ball high and far.

Bowling (*see* top of page opposite) The player holds the ball from below and crouches on one knee, swinging his arm backwards with the ball before swinging through to roll the ball along the ground.

Kicking The conventional techniques such as the push-pass (*see* figure middle left) using the inside part of the foot is adequate for short-range services, while the instep-pass (*see* figure middle right) can be used to kick longer distances. If the service needs to be delivered high, for example to give a player heading practice, then the player serving the ball can gently toss it up in front of himself before playing a volley-pass (*see* bottom figures).

Many of the drills require one of the players to serve the ball to a team-mate to allow him the opportunity to practise and develop his skills. The delivery of the ball needs to be accurate, sensitive and realistic, whether the aim of the drill is to work on controlling, shooting or heading the ball. Remember the maxim, 'poor service starves the practice'.

FOOTBALLS

Many of the drills do not require a lot of balls. However, where possible, the quality should be of the best calibre, with particular attention paid to the size and weight of the balls. For example, when introducing heading to young players, make sure it is a 'pleasure not a pain' for them to prac-tise by using a light ball. Volleyballs are perfect at this stage until the players build up the necessary confidence and technique and can move on to the conventional football. It is a good policy for the coach to have a variety of balls of different sizes, colours, markings, weights and textures. He can then change them depending on the ages of the players, the skills being practised or the difficulty of the drill. The players will progress more quickly, develop greater sensitivity and 'touch' for the ball and generally be more motivated to practise when using a variety of balls.

EQUIPMENT

Self-discipline is part of being a good footballer. Build this quality in your players by getting them into the habit of assisting the coach to set up and take away equipment used in the practice session. Young players like to see an attractive learning environment where portable goals, coloured bibs, cones, varied balls and flag poles are safely set up – it's all part of the fun!

SPACE

The distances and areas mentioned in the book are only approximate. The coach needs to observe how much space and time players require to make the practice drill effective. He should then modify it by positioning the players nearer or farther from each other, or enlarging or reducing the area they are working in. The space will depend on the players' sizes, maturity, ages and skill levels – don't be afraid to change distances when necessary.

The following diagram, which shows one half of a football field, could be utilised by using the flank areas A and B for crossing or long-kicking while C could be used for goalkeeping, shooting or heading. Areas D and E could be used for small-sided games. The centre circle area F could be used for various skills or tactics.

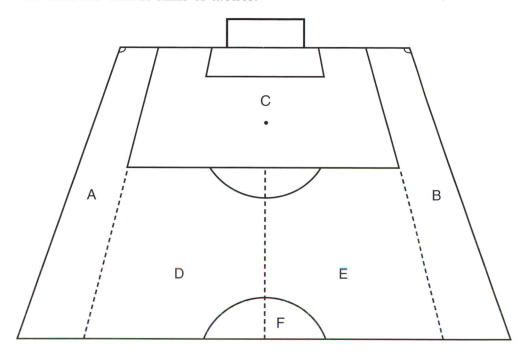

NUMBERS

Ensure that the number of players in each drill is relatively small so that each player has repeated opportunities to practise the skill and improve his ball control. There is nothing worse than having long files of bored youngsters awaiting their turn to perform skills - keep them active! However, the other extreme is for young players to work non-stop and become physically and mentally exhausted. The coach should intersperse the more physically demanding drills with the lighter ones, in order to allow young players to work at their maximum without becoming over-tired.

The drills can be used in a progressive way, working from the easiest to the more difficult. Alternatively, the drills can be varied when the coach thinks fit. However, the same drill should not be used for too long as this can cause boredom. On the whole, youngsters have a shorter attention span than adults, so they do not like 'overcoaching' – it is best to repeat drills often but to keep them short.

Patrick Vieria, the powerful French international midfielder, is a competitive, skilful and influential performer. Modern midfielders need a wide range of technical skills and it is important that they train correctly and are competent on the field in both attacking and defending situations. *Photo: Stu Forster*

Chapter 2

WARMING UP

It is important that young players learn to adopt sensible training habits when attending practice. The first habit the coach needs to instil in them is the need to warm up before they start strenuous physical activity. He should explain to youngsters that there are three reasons for the warm-up:

1 To raise muscle temperature, increase blood flow, stretch the muscles and mobilise the joints of the body. This will allow the players to move through a greater range of movement and will help prevent injury.

2 To maximise performance. The body performs better when demand on the circulatory and respiratory systems increases gradually. Demanding physical activity will fatigue the body prematurely if the body is not warmed up.

3 To prepare mentally. The mind needs to tune in to the practice situation. By rehearsing movement patterns from the game the mind becomes activated and focused on the skills that are needed for practice.

The effective warm-up consists of three phases:

Phase 1 The first phase focuses on getting the whole body mobilised gradually. Light running activities are used to raise the body temperature and heart rate.

Phase 2 The second phase involves stretching the major muscles of the body and the joints. Particular attention should be paid to specific muscles and joints that are used in playing the game, i.e. the spine, hips, and legs.

Phase 3 The third, and final, phase is the most intensive and involves activities performed at a faster tempo that allow players to practise and rehearse patterns of movements from the games. Note: players should do some light running after the stretches in phase 2 to raise the heart rate and temperature before starting this phase.

By the end of these three phases the players will be ready mentally and physically to get the best from the practice drills. Most coaches have enough material to carry out phases 1 and 2 competently, so the drills provided in this chapter are specifically designed for phase 3 of the warm-up.

Drill 1

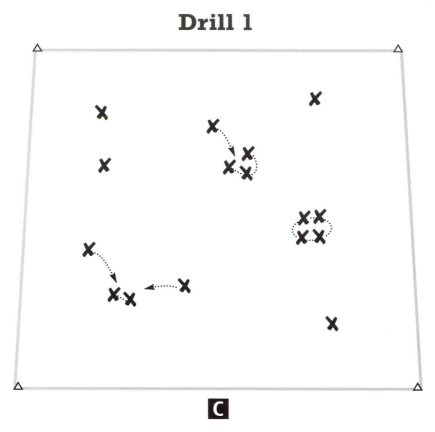

Purpose: Reactions and changing direction

Practice set-up: A group of players runs around inside a 20 yd square, changing speed and direction. The coach suddenly calls a number (e.g. 'Four') and the players must bond as quickly as possible to form groups of the number called. They bond with each other by holding hands to form an unbreakable chain or by putting their arms around each other's shoulders. The odd ones out who were last to bond have to do a fun forfeit (e.g. 3 star jumps). The players then run again and the coach calls a new number.

Equipment: Four cones

Progressions: The coach can put increased pressure on the players by pointing to one of the four lines of the square whereby they have to run to the *opposite* line, or asking them to perform different movements before they 'bond' (e.g. move sideways, move backwards etc.).

Drill 2

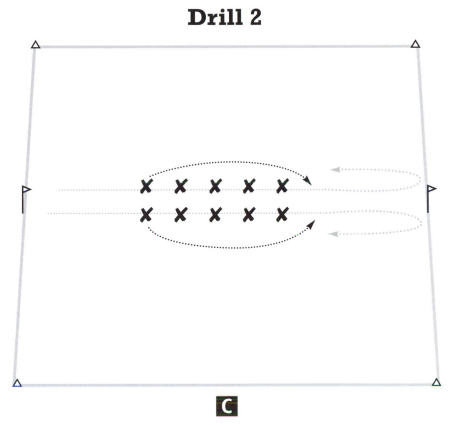

Purpose: Aerobic preparation and change of speed

Practice set-up: The players form two files a yard apart from each other in a channel marked with two poles 20 yds apart. The players jog together towards each flag pole, turning at the same time and jogging in the opposite direction towards the other pole. The coach whistles and the two back players sprint to the front of the file where they continue to jog slowly. The next pair at the back await the coach's signal for them to sprint forwards.

Equipment: Four cones, two flag poles

Progressions: The coach can change the drill by asking the front players, as they are jogging forwards, to turn and sprint to the back of the file. He can also ask the players sprinting to run backwards or sideways, or increase the work tempo so that the players perform more sprints.

Drill 3

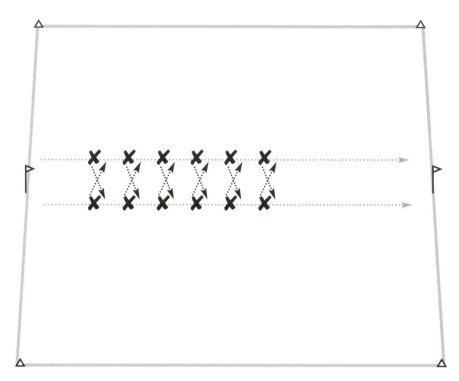

Purpose: Aerobic work and lateral movement

Practice set-up: Two files of players stand 2 yds apart in a channel marked with two flag poles 20 yds apart. As in drill 2, they keep in a line and jog up and down between the poles. On the coach's whistle each person in the file quickly changes position with the person opposite, moving laterally. The two files then carry on jogging as before, awaiting the next whistle, upon which they change at speed once again. Players should not cross their legs over when they change positions.

Equipment: Four cones, two flag poles

Progressions: The coach calls a number between 1 and 3 as the two files of players jog forwards. The players must respond by quickly changing places with the player opposite in a zig-zag fashion for the required number of times. At the same time they still move forwards in unison. When they are finished changing places the files carry on jogging alongside each other until the next number is called.

Drill 4

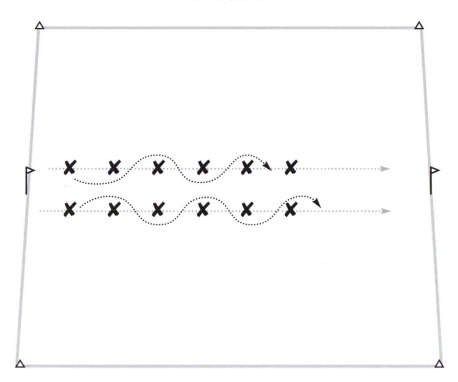

Purpose: Changing direction

Practice set-up: Two files of players stand 2 yds apart from each other, with each player the same distance from the player behind and/or in front. A channel is marked by two flag poles, which are 20 yds apart. The players jog in files backwards and forwards between the poles. The coach whistles and the two back players race each other to the front. As they do so they run in and out of each player in the file.

Equipment: Four cones, two flag poles

Progressions: The coach can change the format by asking the front players to race to the back by moving backwards in and out of the file and joining the end of the file.

Drill 5

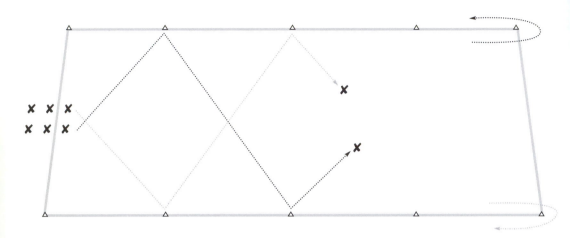

Purpose: Changing direction

Practice set-up: In an area measuring 40 yds long by 15 yds wide, four or five cones are placed on the outside lines 10 yds apart. Two files of players stand close together between two cones at one end and run in pairs on the coach's command, running wide to touch the cones and crossing in the middle *at the same time* until they have completed the run. They then run straight down the outside line to re-join their file as the next two players set out.

Equipment: Ten cones

Progressions: The coach can mix up the movements as the players run between cones (e.g. ask them to move forwards, sideways, backwards, or to hop etc.).

Drill 6

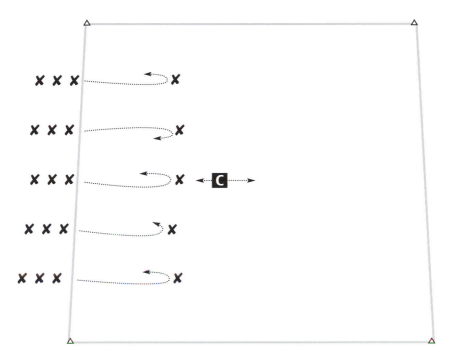

Purpose: Change of speed and direction

Practice set-up: Files of 4–6 players stand in a line facing the coach, who is 10 yds away in a 25 yd square. The coach, who can move forwards or backwards in the area, first moves backwards slowly, which is a signal for the first players from each file to run towards him. As soon as the coach stops, the line of players races to line up with him, then turns quickly and runs back towards the starting line. As the players are running back to the starting line with their backs to him, the coach changes position. When the players reach the line, they turn and run to where the coach has repositioned himself, until they have completed 3–5 runs. The next line of players sets off immediately, so that the drill continues and each group has a recovery period. The first players back each time can be awarded points.

Equipment: Four cones

Progressions: Increase the length, number or type of runs that the players have to make (e.g. ask them to run backwards, sideways etc.).

Drill 7

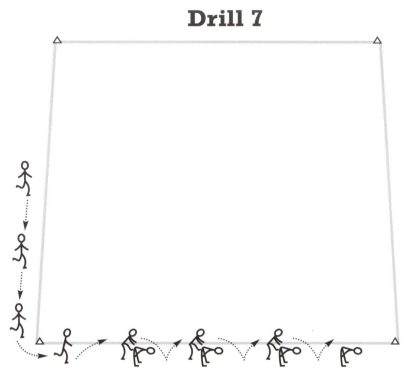

Purpose: Aerobic work, agility and leg power

Practice set-up: In a 20 yd square a file of players starts jogging around the perimeter, each player about 3–5 yds apart. On the coach's whistle, the front player stops and 'makes a back' by bending over at the waist with the legs astride and hands resting above the knees for extra support, making sure he is a suitable height to be jumped over. The player following approaches him and, placing both hands on the first player's back, leapfrogs over him and runs forwards to make a 'back' himself. After leapfrogging, all the players make a 'back' for the players following to leapfrog. The first player then leapfrogs through the file until he is at the front again. The file then starts jogging around the perimeter of the square until the coach whistles again. The coach varies the distance they jog depending on the fitness of the group and the length of the warm-up required. Ensure heavy boys do not leap over boys who are obviously too light to support them.

Equipment: Four cones

Progressions: Increase the number of times the drill is performed and the jogging distance between drills.

Drill 8

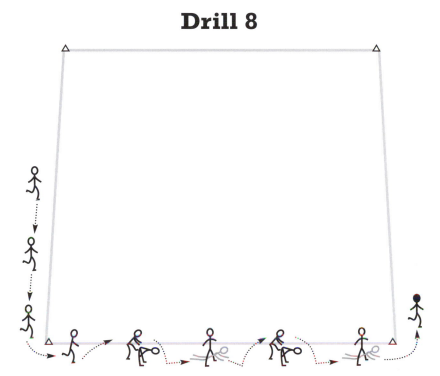

Purpose: Aerobic running, agility and jumping

Practice set-up: A file of players jogs around a 20 yd square as in drill 7. This time, on the coach's whistle the players alternately leapfrog over a team-mate's back and then crawl quickly under and through the outstretched legs of the next player. They commence the over-and-under sequence in the same way as drill 7, with the front player making a back first etc., but this time the third player will leapfrog the first player and crawl through the second player and so on. The file then starts jogging around the square until the coach whistles again. The sequence of over-and-under continues for a prescribed time or number of circuits around the square. Ensure that players leapfrog safely and correctly.

Equipment: Four cones

Progressions: Increase the tempo, or add more circuits around the square.

Drill 9

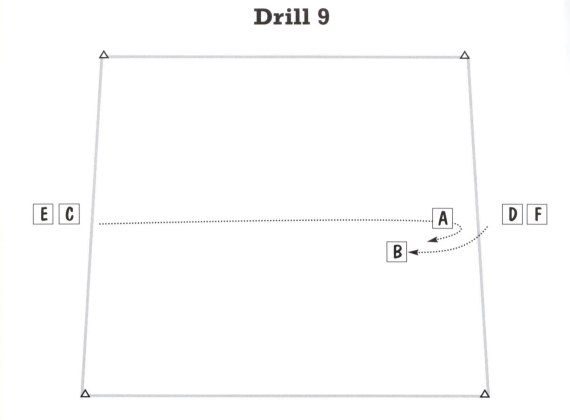

Purpose: More demanding aerobic activity and turning at speed

Practice set-up: Two files of players face each other 15-25 yds apart. The first player, A, runs on his own to the other side to join the opposite file. As he gets near the opposite line, player B from the opposite file sets off running past player A. Player A now slows down, turns quickly and gives chase to B and then joins player B's file. As player B nears the opposite side, player C sets off past him, and player B now turns to chase him. In this way each player is chased by another player before chasing another player himself on the way back to his own file. The drill continues in sequence so that each player gets a recovery period.

Equipment: Four cones

Progressions: The coach can ask the player to chase in a normal forward direction, but to run backwards or sideways when he is being chased – this will make the exercise more competitive.

Drill 10

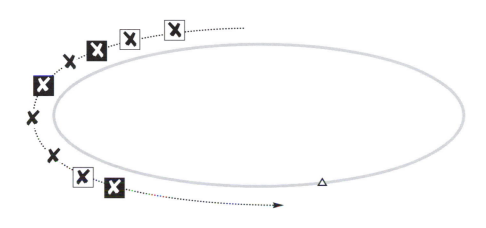

Purpose: More demanding aerobic activity and short sprints

Practice set-up: A group of players jogs around the centre circle, which has a cone placed on it. The group should keep together, although if the coach wishes it could be split into smaller teams with coloured bibs to identify the different players. As they jog up to the cone, the coach whistles and the group races around the circle to see who is last past the cone. The last one drops out and the group jogs slowly around again, jogging on the spot at the cone before sprinting again on the coach's whistle. The last one past the cone drops out again – the last player left wins.

Equipment: One cone

Progressions: The coach can increase the size of the circle, or give each player two or three chances. If a player comes last three times, he has lost all of his chances and must drop out.

Chapter 3

DRIBBLING AND RUNNING WITH THE BALL

Players in this age group will be becoming more sophisticated, co-ordinated and stronger in their movements, which will allow them to be more adventurous in their approach to the game. They can now move much more quickly and accurately with the ball at their feet and can solidify their techniques and 'tricks' which should be wide-ranging. They also need to learn that dribbling or running with the ball is a means to an end and not just something to be performed for the sake of it. This requires judgement and deciding when, and when not, to dribble or run with the ball.

Opposite: **Brian Laudrup, the Danish forward, uses his exceptional technical skills to create havoc with even the best organised defences. He is particularly adept at running at defenders with the ball, wrong-footing them, then cleverly dodging past them.** *Photo: Laurent Zabulon*

Drill 11

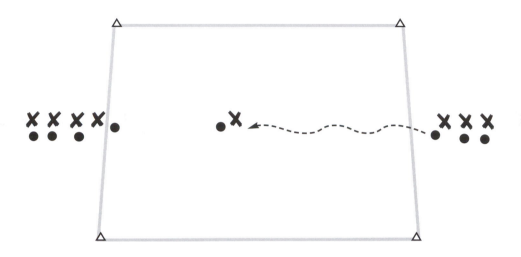

Purpose: Running with the ball at speed

Practice set-up: Two files of players stand slightly to the side but facing each other 12–15 yds apart, with a ball each at their feet. The first player in a file proceeds to run in a straight line with the ball. When he dribbles it across the opposite line, the first player in the opposite file sets off with the ball at his feet in the opposite direction, to create momentum in the exercise. The players should practise using both feet, increasing the tempo or running over a longer area so they cover more distance with the ball.

Equipment: Four cones, one ball per player

Progressions: This drill can be executed with one ball only – each player stops the ball with the sole of his foot and it is left for the next player to take it up.

Drill 12

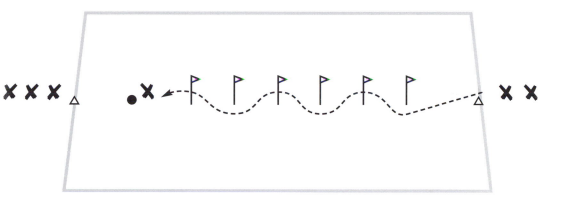

Purpose: Running and dribbling in a restricted area

Practice set-up: The group of players is broken into files of players who compete against each other via slalom courses, marked with poles placed on the ground 1–3 yds apart. Each file splits into two, with half the file at one end of a slalom course, and the other half at the other end. Each player, in turn, dribbles the ball through the cones in a fashion designated by the coach (e.g. left foot only, alternate feet or some other prescribed technique) before his team-mate takes over from other the side. Each player has to carry out a set number of dribbles and the first team to finish the course wins.

Equipment: Two cones, six to eight flag poles

Progressions: The tempo can be increased or the slalom course made harder by placing the poles closer together.

Drill 13

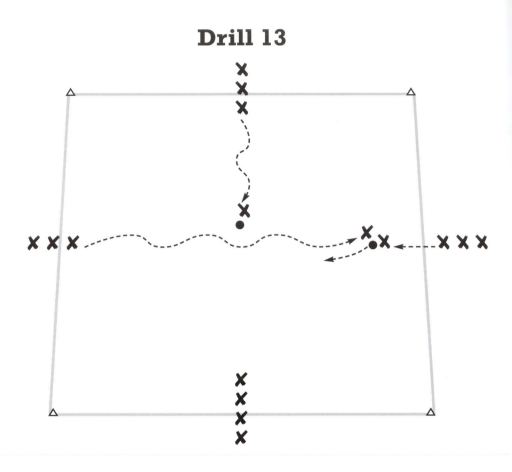

Purpose: 'Take-overs' and running with the ball

Practice set-up: Four files of players form a cross formation with each file 15–25 yds apart. Two adjacent files have a ball each. Each player in turn runs with the ball to the opposite file where the next player performs a 'take-over' by taking the ball and dribbling it across to the opposite file. The players must take care to avoid each other as they move at speed with the ball at their feet.

Equipment: Two balls

Progressions: Increase the size of the area so the players need to run with the ball for a longer period.

Drill 14

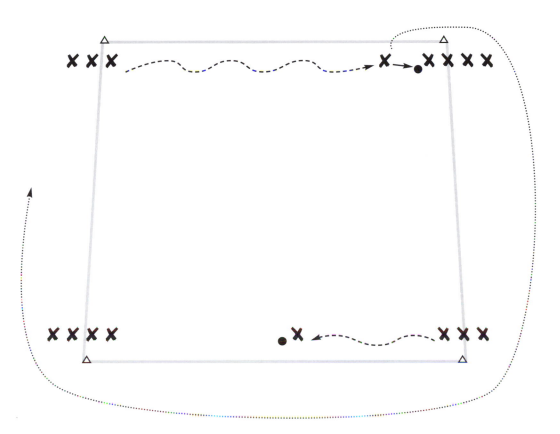

Purpose: Running with and without the ball

Practice set-up: Four files of players line up at the corners of a 20 yd square. Two files that are diagonally opposite have a ball each. The first players run with the ball across to a file without a ball, leaving it with the next player. The first players then jog without the ball around the square (making sure that they run the *longest* way around) until they reach their original file.

Equipment: Four cones, two balls

Progressions: As the drill progresses, the coach can add a ball to the other two files and four players set off at the same time to speed up the practice.

Drill 15

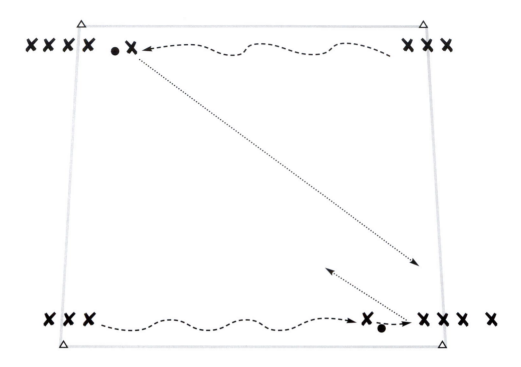

Purpose: Running with the ball and changing direction

Practice set-up: Four files of players line up in the corners of a 20 yd square marked out with cones. Two files that are diagonally opposite have a ball each. As in drill 14, the first player in two of the files dribbles the ball across to the opposite file, where he stops the ball for the next player. This time, however, he runs to the file diagonally opposite as the next player continues the drill.

Equipment: Four cones, two balls

Progressions: As in drill 14, the coach adds a ball to the other two files and four players set off at the same time to speed up the practice.

Drill 16

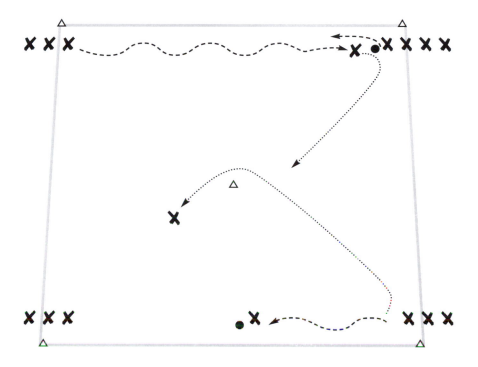

Purpose: Running with the ball and quick changes of direction

Practice set-up: As in drills 14 and 15, four files of players stand at the corners of a 20 yd square, and the first players in two diagonally opposite files have a ball. A cone is placed in the centre of the square. The players with the balls dribble the balls across to the opposite file, leaving them in the possession of the next players. They continue running, but this time without the ball, back around the central cone to rejoin the back of their original file. Each player completes the exercise at a fast pace.

Equipment: Five cones, two balls

Progressions: The coach can ask players to use one foot only when dribbling or turning with the ball, or to perform a 'trick' as he moves at speed with the ball.

Drill 17

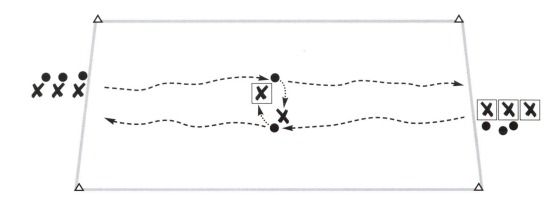

Purpose: Running, stopping and turning with the ball

Practice set-up: Two files of players stand 15–20 yds apart, facing each other, but positioned a yard to the side of each other. Each player has a ball at his feet. The first two players dribble the ball to the centre, aiming to arrive next to each other at the same time. When they meet at the centre, they put the sole of their foot on their ball, bringing it to a halt. They then step quickly to the side, leaving their own ball and dribbling their partner's ball back to their own file. The next two players from each file repeat the exercise.

Equipment: Four cones, a good supply of balls, one set of coloured bibs

Progressions: The coach can create a competition in which teams, each comprising two files of players, speed up and try to complete a given number of runs with the ball before the other team.

Drill 18

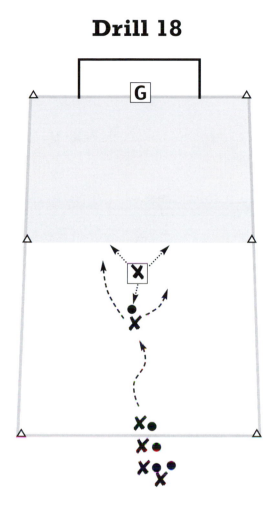

Purpose: Dribbling past an opponent

Practice set-up: A channel 10-12 yds wide by 15-20 yds long is marked out. A goalkeeper is positioned in front of the goal at one end, facing a line of players. Each player has a ball. One defender stands facing them. A 'no-tackling' zone is marked out 6-8 yds from the goal which the defender cannot enter. The players come forwards one at a time to try and dribble their ball past the defender and score.

Equipment: Six cones, a good supply of balls

Progressions: The coach times the drill for a set period before changing the players over so that someone else becomes the defender.

Drill 19

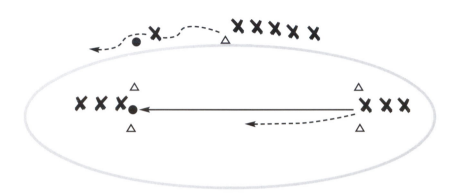

Purpose: Running at speed with the ball and short passing

Practice set-up: Two groups of 4-6 players are assembled. One group forms a file standing outside the centre circle with a ball at the front player's feet, while the other group breaks into two files who face each other 15 yds apart and inside the circle. Cones are placed 10 yds wide and on both sides of the files to mark a channel between then. On the coach's whistle, the outside players take it in turns to dribble the ball around the circle as quickly as possible. Meanwhile, the central players pass the ball to the opposite file, then run to join the end of the opposite file. The players passing the ball must control it each time. However, each player must allow the ball to pass *through* his cones before passing it back to another player. The central players should count how many passes were made before all the dribbling players got around the circle.

Equipment: Five cones, two balls

Progressions: The teams change and try to beat the other's passing record. (The team with the most passes wins because it means the other team took longer to run with the ball around the centre circle.)

Drill 20

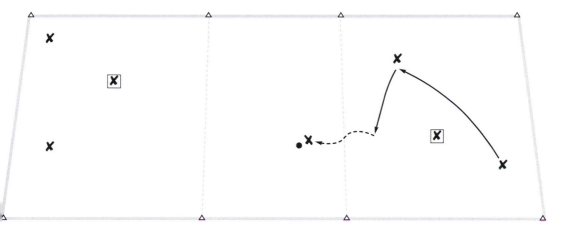

Purpose: Running with the ball and decision-making

Practice set-up: A channel measuring 40 yds long by 15 yds wide is marked out. Two 15 yd squares are marked out at the ends of this area. In one square there is a 3 vs 1 situation with three attackers and one defender; in the other square there is a 2 vs 1 situation with two attackers and one defender. One of the attackers in the first square looks to have enough space to dribble the ball through the middle zone and into the other square to link up with the other two attackers, making a 3 vs 1 situation once again. The defenders are not allowed to enter the middle zone and the ball cannot be passed into this area either: the players must dribble the ball into the middle zone. The action carries on from end to end, with a player running with the ball through the middle zone to link up at the other end.

Equipment: Eight cones, one ball

Progressions: The coach can add another defender in the longer central zone. The attacker must dribble the ball past this player before linking up with the end players. The defender adopts a passive, obstructive role at first, but is allowed to tackle as the drill progresses.

Chapter 4

PASSING THE BALL

Young players in this age range are becoming physically stronger and more mature, so their range of passing techniques can be extended. They should still spend a lot of time practising passes without opponents, to improve their techniques. They also need some drill practices involving opponents, which will enable them to learn about where and when to use their passing techniques in a real game.

Zinedine Zidane, the high-class French midfield 'General', fulfilled his outstanding potential with a marvellous World Cup performance on his home soil in 1998. His ability to create openings for his colleagues with his range of passing skills was magical and made a massive contribution to his team's success. *Photo: Christophe Guibbaud*

Drill 21

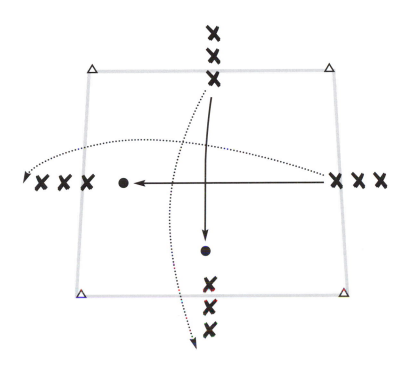

Purpose: Short passing and controlled movement of the ball

Practice set-up: Four files of players line up 8–12 yds apart in a cross formation. The first players in two adjacent files have a ball at their feet and face the file directly opposite. Both players look to pass the ball across to the first player in the opposite file and to run after it, trying to make sure they do not collide with another ball or player before joining the end of the opposite file. Each player, in turn, controls and passes the ball so the drill flows.

Equipment: Four cones, two balls

Progressions: The coach can restrict players to first-time passes where possible, or allow players to play different types of passes (e.g. instep, chipped or outside of the foot).

Drill 22

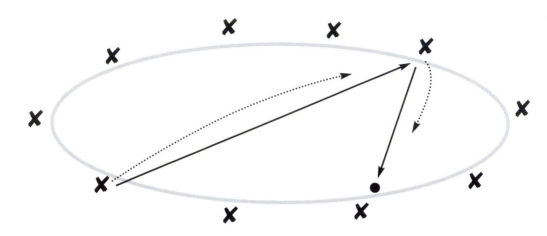

Purpose: Short passing and controlled movement of the ball

Practice set-up: A group of players stand, evenly spaced, around the centre circle or similar area. One player has the ball at his feet. He passes the ball across the circle and follows it directly to change positions with the player receiving the pass. Each player passes, follows the ball and changes positions, increasing the tempo as the drill progresses.

Equipment: One to three balls

Progressions: Eventually add a second or third ball, so that more players are involved and the difficulty is increased.

Drill 23

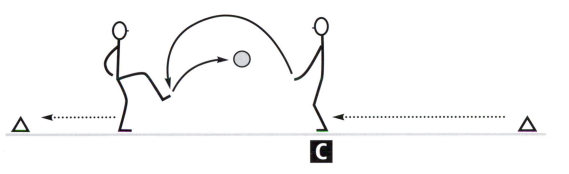

Purpose: Short volley and moving in a backward direction

Practice set-up: A player faces the coach 3-8 yds away. The coach holds a ball. Starting at a cone, the coach proceeds to serve the ball to the player by tossing it in the air underarm so that the player can return the ball by volleying it back for the coach to catch. The coach keeps moving forwards, forcing the player to move backwards for each volley.

Equipment: Two cones, one ball

Progressions: While the coach keeps the player on the move in a backward direction, the player volleys the ball either with one foot at a time or alternates between left and right.

Drill 24

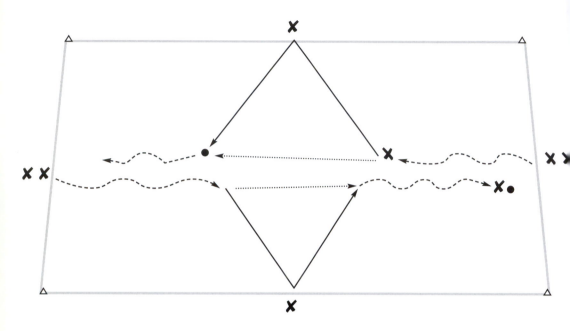

Purpose: Wall-passing

Practice set-up: Two files of players face each other at the ends of an area measuring 30 yds long by 15 yds wide. Two other players stand halfway between the files and opposite each other. They are positioned at the edge of the area and wide apart. The first player in each file plays the ball to the wide player on the right – a wall-pass. The wide player returns a first-time pass to the passer, who runs on to receive the ball. The passer then dribbles the ball to the oncoming file. The next player then plays a wall-pass with the wide player on his right side.

Equipment: Four cones, two balls

Progressions: As the drill progresses, the coach can introduce another ball so the wall-passes can be played from both sides simultaneously.

Drill 25

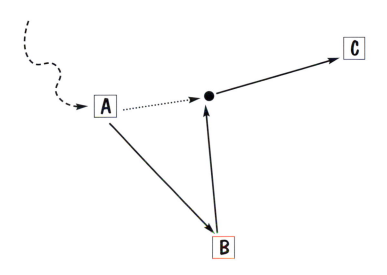

Purpose: Wall-passing to set up play

Practice set-up: Three players stand 5–8 yds apart in a triangle with one of them in possession of the ball. Player A runs with the ball towards Player B and plays a wall-pass (for reference *see* drill 24). After player A receives the ball from player B he passes the ball to player C, who is now positioned a bit further away. Player C then runs with the ball to player A and plays a wall-pass before passing to player B, who repeats the same process.

Equipment: One ball

Progressions: The three players speed up the tempo as they gain more confidence in their passing skills.

Drill 26

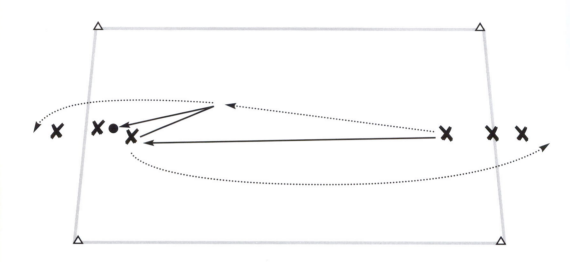

Purpose: Setting up passes

Practice set-up: Two files of players stand 12–20 yds apart and face each other. The first player in one file has the ball at his feet. He passes the ball directly across to the first player in the opposite file, then follows it to receive a short first-time pass from that player. After receiving the ball, the first player plays a short pass to the next player in the file and then joins the end of the opposite file. The player with the ball then proceeds to set up a pass for the player at the far end and so the drill continues. After the final pass, the first player joins the end of the file.

Equipment: Four cones, one ball

Progressions: The coach can ask the player passing the ball to the opposite file to chip the ball in the air so that the receiving player can either control the ball or play a little volley back to him.

Drill 27

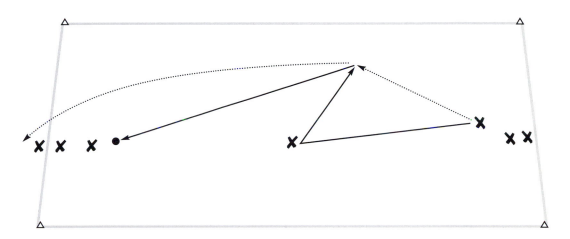

Purpose: Setting up play

Practice set-up: Two files of players stand 30–40 yds apart, with one player standing in the middle. The first player in one file has the ball at his feet. The player with the ball passes it to the middle player and follows up to receive a short, angled pass from him before passing to the first player in the opposite file. He then joins the opposite file as the next player starts to play. The middle player is the 'setting-up' player for the players in the files as they move from end to end.

Equipment: Four cones, one ball

Progressions: The coach can restrict the players to two touches only, so that the passing and control is crisp and quick.

Drill 28

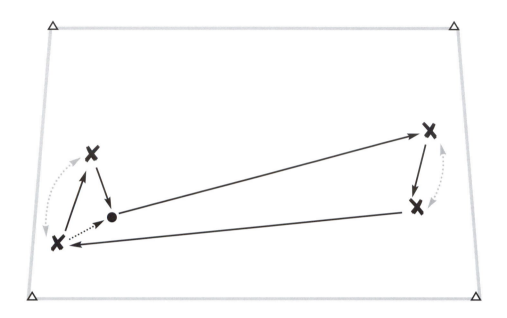

Purpose: Setting up play

Practice set-up: Players position themselves in pairs at each end of a channel measuring 20 yds long by 12 yds wide. The player with the ball passes it to one of the players at the other end, who cushions it for his partner. The player receiving the ball plays a short, angled pass to his partner, who passes the ball to the other player at the far end of the channel. The pairs of players interchange after passing the ball to the players opposite and look to set up play for each other.

Equipment: Four cones, one ball

Progressions: The coach can restrict the players to two touches or even one touch if the players can cope with this. Alternatively, the coach can ask the player passing to the opposite file to chip or drive the ball to increase the difficulty.

Drill 29

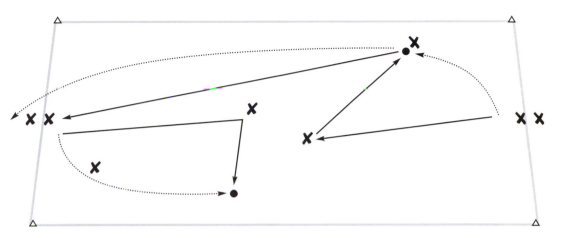

Purpose: Setting up passes

Practice set-up: Two files of players stand at opposite ends of a channel measuring 30 yds long by 15 yds wide. Two players stand in the middle. The first player in each file has a ball at his feet and proceeds to pass it to one of the middle players, then he runs wide to receive a cushioned return pass. After receiving the return pass he plays a through pass to the next player in the opposite file and then runs to the back of that file. The coach should ensure that both middle players pass to the same side (i.e. their left or right) each time and that the drill flows with rhythmic passing.

Equipment: Four cones, two balls

Progressions: The coach can restrict the players to one- or two-touch play.

Drill 30

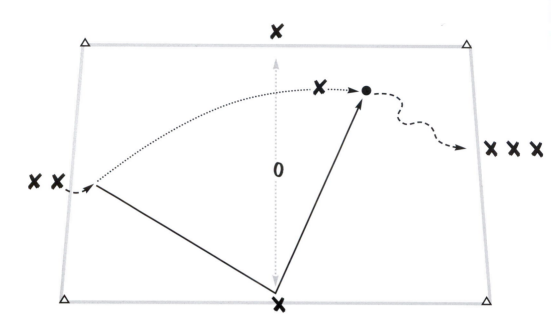

Purpose: Wall-passing

Practice set-up: Two files of players stand at opposite ends of a channel measuring 15–20 yds long by 12 yds wide. The first player in one file has the ball. Two other players stand halfway and on the edges of the channel. A defender stands in the centre. The first player comes forwards with the ball and looks to play a wall-pass to either of the wide players in an attempt to get past the defender. The defender can move along the halfway line to challenge for the ball. After receiving the return pass, he dribbles the ball to the first player in the opposite file. The drill then carries on from the other side, and the defender turns around to face the next player. The two wide players can change their positions to enable the wall-pass to be achieved.

Equipment: Four cones, one or two balls

Progressions: The coach can restrict wall-passing to one-touch only. The defender should be changed at regular intervals. An extra ball can be added to speed up the practice.

Drill 31

Purpose: Control and touch of the ball

Practice set-up: Three players stand 2-3 yds apart to form a triangle. One player has the ball. He gently tosses the ball to a team-mate, who gently volleys the ball to himself or to another player. The players look to keep the ball in the air with volleys and they should try and alternate their feet.

Equipment: One ball

Progressions: To progress, each player can juggle the ball with his feet for a set number of times before volleying it to another player for him to do likewise – players should count the number of touches and/or volleys that they manage. Use balls of different sizes, weights and textures and have groups compete against other groups to see who can keep the ball up longest.

Drill 32

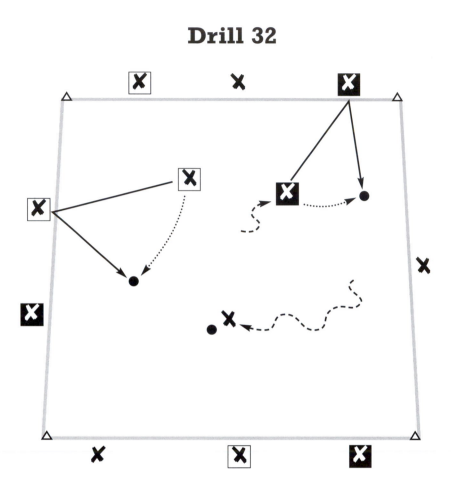

Purpose: Wall-passing and running with the ball

Practice set-up: A square measuring 15 by 15 yds, or circle of equivalent size, is marked out. Three groups of three or four players, dressed in different coloured bibs, are positioned and spread out around the area. One player from each group is placed inside the area, each with a ball. These players dribble around inside the area and play wall-passes (for reference *see* drill 24) continually with their team-mates for a set time. They then change places with another player from their team.

Equipment: Four cones, a good supply of balls, sets of coloured bibs

Progressions: The coach can restrict players to one-touch when they actually play the wall-pass.

Drill 33

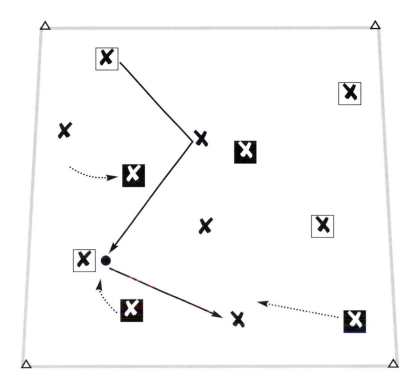

Purpose: Running with the ball and wall-passing

Practice set-up: A square measuring 15 yds by 15 yds is marked out. Three teams of four or five players, wearing different coloured bibs, play possession football with two teams playing together against the other team (e.g. 8 vs 4) each time. When a team's players give possession away, that team has to defend against the other two teams.

Equipment: Three sets of coloured bibs, four cones, one ball

Progressions: The teams play competitively and try and attain the highest passing sequence.

Drill 34

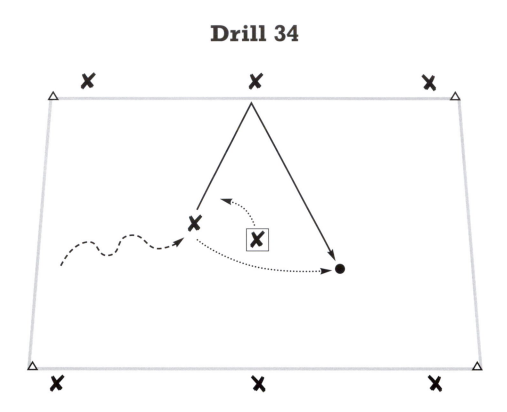

Purpose: Running with the ball and wall-passing

Practice set-up: An area measuring 20 yds long by 12 yds wide is marked out to form a channel. Six players, three on each of the long sides, stand outside the area. An attacker and a defender stand at one end of the channel. The attacker starts with the ball at his feet and dribbles around the area looking to play a wall-pass, with any of the six players, which would enable him to get to the other end with the ball. He must do this within a time limit. The defender looks to intercept or tackle the attacker to win the ball. If the player manages to get past the defender with two passes, he then starts from the other end and looks to move back past the defender again.

Equipment: Four cones, one coloured bib, one ball

Progressions: Change players after a set time and count the number of successful wall-passes for each player.

Drill 35

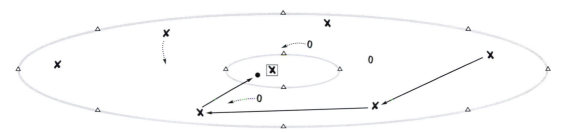

Purpose: Passing and switching play by passing the ball from one side of the field to the other

Practice set-up: A circle with a 25 yd radius is set up, containing an inner circle with a 3–5 yd radius. One player stands in the inner circle. Five or six attackers play possession football in the outer circle against three defenders. The object of the play is for one of the attackers to pass the ball to the player in the inner circle, thereby gaining a point. All the players must stay in the outer circle and cannot enter the inner circle apart from the designated player, who cannot leave it. Defenders can run temporarily through the inner circle, but if they stop a pass in there, they give away a point. Change players over and count the points scored.

Equipment: Cones to mark the circles, one ball

Progressions: Add another defender or decrease the size of the outer circle a little to put pressure on the passing.

Chapter 5

SHOOTING AT GOAL

Coaches have an important part to play when introducing and developing this skill with young players. Many youngsters begin to develop bad habits quite early on in their career when shooting at goal because they believe that power is more important than accuracy. The result is that they become excited, slash at the ball, and miss the target. They should be encouraged to be creative when shooting and learn to outwit the goalkeeper by using various techniques to beat him. These may include chipped shots over his head or shots that bend around him, as well as the power-drive!

Dwight Yorke, the ever-smiling Trinidadian, is a class act. He has all the hallmarks of a top goal-scorer, including confidence and calmness. His high goal-tally is testimony to his skill in this area of the game. *Photo: Clive Brunskill*

Drill 36

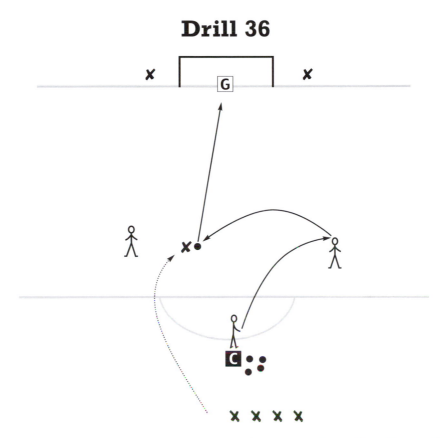

Purpose: To shoot at goal with a high-service, through-volley or half-volley

Practice set-up: The coach stands outside the penalty area with a supply of balls and faces the goalkeeper. Two ball-retrievers stand at the back of the goal. In front of and to the sides of the coach, two players stand 10–15 yds away. A file of players stands 10 yds behind the coach. The coach tosses the ball high in the air. One of the players in front of the coach side-heads the ball accurately for the first player in the file, who breaks away, gets to the ball and shoots at goal. He might hit the ball on the volley or control it before striking. The player returns to the back of the file as the coach tosses the ball up for another player in front to head, thus setting up the shot for the next player in the file.

Equipment: A good supply of balls

Progressions: The coach can restrict the players to one or two touches.

Drill 37

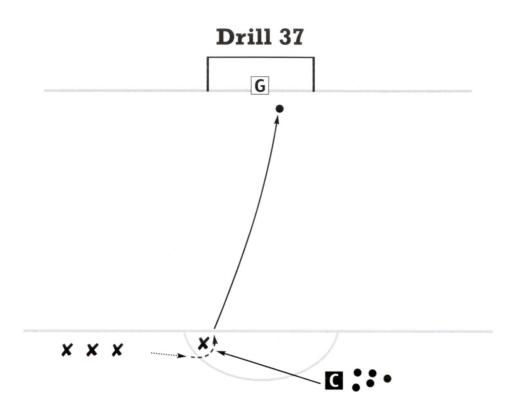

Purpose: Turning to shoot at goal

Practice set-up: The coach stands behind the penalty area and in front and slightly to the side of a file of players. The coach serves the ball to the first player by throwing it in the air or passing it along the ground. The player controls the ball and turns quickly with it to shoot at goal. The service should be given to both sides so that the players get practice in using both feet and different techniques.

Equipment: A good supply of balls

Progressions: The coach can restrict players to one or two touches, or ask players to cushion the ball in the air when they control it before volleying at goal.

Drill 38

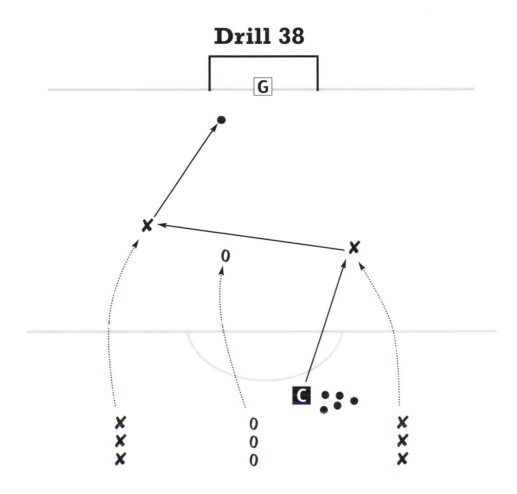

Purpose: Deciding to shoot, or to give a team-mate a chance at goal

Practice set-up: Three files of players stand 5–8 yds apart outside the penalty area and facing the goal. The coach stands in a central position in front of the files with a good supply of balls. He passes the ball in turn to one of the players from the outside files. The player nearest to the ball looks to shoot at goal or drag the ball across for the other attacking team-mate to score. The middle player always acts as a defender and tries to stop the shot each time.

Equipment: A good supply of balls

Progressions: The coach can serve the ball more unpredictably to players to increase the pressure on their shooting skills.

Drill 39

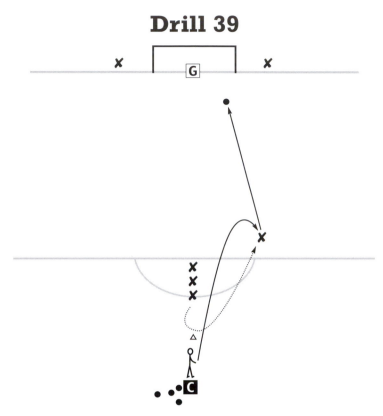

Purpose: Turning to shoot on the volley

Practice set-up: A file of players lines up at the edge of the penalty area, facing a cone positioned 6 yds away from the penalty area. The goalkeeper stands in the goal and a ball-retriever stands on each side of the goal. The coach, who has a good supply of balls, is positioned a few yards further on. The first player runs towards the cone and as soon as he reaches it, he receives a tossed high-service from the coach that just passes over his head. He turns quickly and gets to the ball to volley it at goal. The coach serves the balls at a fast pace and is helped by the two ball retrievers behind the goal who maintain the flow and circulation of the balls.

Equipment: One cone, a good supply of balls

Progressions: The coach only allows the ball to bounce twice before the players shoot on the half-volley. As they improve, it can be one bounce only or even no bounces, so that the player hits the ball at the goal before it drops to make contact with the ground.

Drill 40

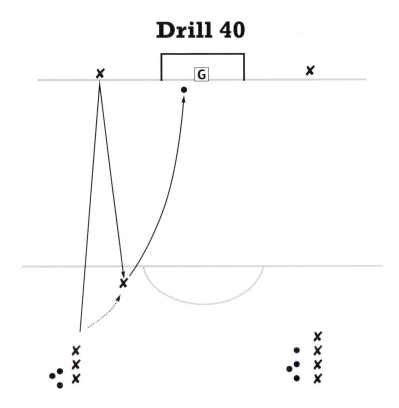

Purpose: Shooting at goal from a pass to your feet

Practice set-up: Two files of players face two players positioned on the touchlines 25–30 yds away and on each side of the goal. Each file has a good supply of balls. A player from one file strikes a firm pass to the far player on the touchline and follows it up to hit the return pass first-time at goal. Play then originates from the other file and the drill continues with the files alternating.

Equipment: A good supply of balls

Progressions: The files change places so that they gain practice with both feet and from both sides of the field. Players should remember to strike the top half of the ball to keep the shot down.

Drill 41

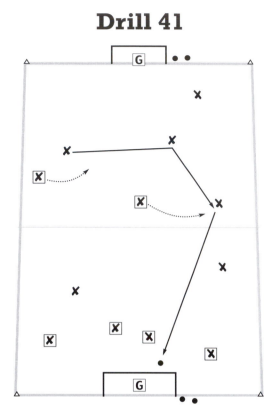

Purpose: Long-range shooting

Practice set-up: Two portable goals are set up in an area 30 yds long by 20 yds wide. Each goal is guarded by a goalkeeper. Two teams of six players, including four attackers and two defenders, play in each half of the field and they cannot leave their area. The four attackers look to set up chances to shoot in the other team's goal, while the two defenders challenge for the ball. The drill starts with one of the goalkeepers rolling the ball to the team in his half. During play the two defenders also attack if they intercept the ball from either the attackers or a rebound from their own team.

Equipment: Four cones, two portable goals, two sets of coloured bibs, a few balls

Progressions: Make the drill more competitive by totalling the goal scores of the teams, or add an extra defender to each team.

Drill 42

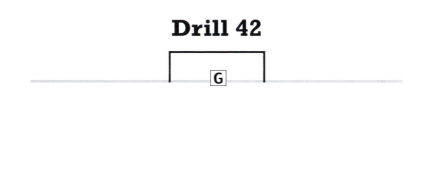

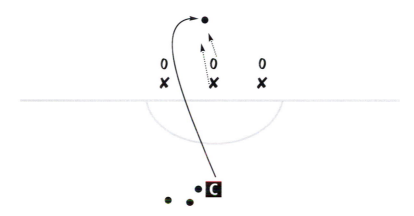

Purpose: Turning to shoot at goal

Practice set-up: Three attacking players stand on the penalty area facing the coach, who is positioned 6–10 yds away, with a good supply of balls. Three defenders mark the attacking players, but they face the goal and are not allowed to turn and look at the ball until it is served. The coach tosses the ball through or over the players and the players nearest the ball give chase, either trying to score or prevent the shot. The attackers have an advantage by seeing the ball earlier. The coach serves another new ball as soon as the players have reformed.

Equipment: A good supply of balls

Progressions: The coach can vary the service or create a competition among the different players to see who scores the most goals.

Drill 43

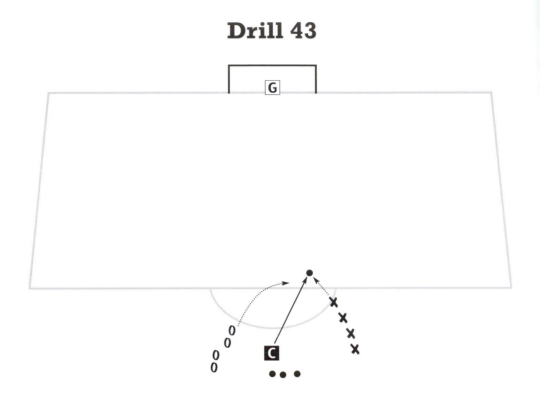

Purpose: To shoot accurately with a recovering defender

Practice set-up: Two files of players, one attacking and the other defending, stand facing the goal and goalkeeper. The coach stands between the two files. The attackers start a few yards ahead of the defenders. The coach serves the ball in a variety of ways to the attackers while the defenders try to prevent shots at goal. The files change roles, always ensuring that the attacking players have an advantage.

Equipment: A good supply of balls

Progressions: The defenders can be brought a little nearer to the attackers to make the shooting situation even harder.

Drill 44

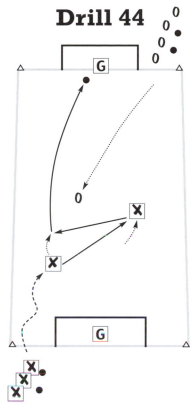

Purpose: Using an extra man to get in a shot at goal

Practice set-up: Two goals are erected, each defended by a goalkeeper, in an area measuring 18 yds long by 10 yds wide. Two files of players stand on opposite sides of each goal with a good supply of balls. Two players emerge from one file with a ball while one player comes from the other file to act as a defender. They play 2 vs 1 and the attackers try to score. The lone defender tries to prevent this. The players return to their files and another 2 vs 1 situation emerges, but this time the two attackers come from the opposite file. The drill alternates from end to end.

Equipment: Four cones, two portable goals, two sets of coloured bibs, a good supply of balls

Progressions: The coach can create a 2 vs 2 situation where an extra defender emerges each time. Alternatively, the defender can play offside in the 2 vs 1 situation, so that the two attackers need to time their runs and passes before shooting.

Drill 45

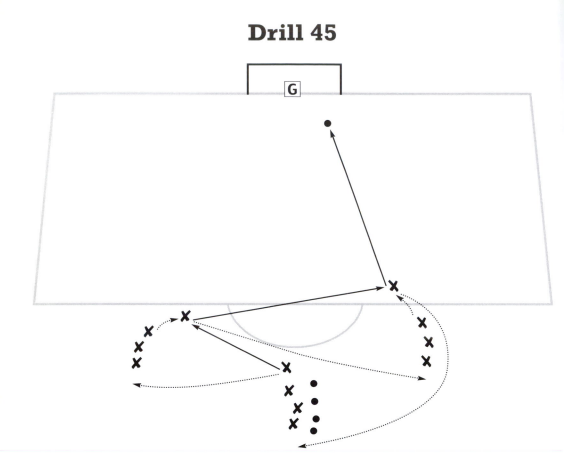

Purpose: Various shooting situations

Practice set-up: Three files of players stand in a row outside the penalty area with the middle file slightly further back. The middle file has a good supply of balls. The first player in the middle file passes the ball to the file on his left whose player passes it to the first player in the far right file, who immediately shoots at goal. All three players rotate clockwise and the drill continues with the next three players. The passes and shots can also be played in the opposite direction.

Equipment: A good supply of balls

Progressions: The coach can vary the direction of the passes and therefore the shots at goal (e.g. pass and turn to shoot, pass in front of player to shoot or pass back to oncoming player to shoot).

Drill 46

Purpose: Various shooting situations

Practice set-up: A channel is marked from the lines on the outside of the penalty area to the halfway line. Six balls are laid inside the centre circle. Teams play 4 vs 4 football. The team that has possession of the ball looks to shoot and score while the other team tries to stop them. As soon as a team has a shot, the other team immediately sends one of their players to dribble and fetch the next ball as they, in turn, attack the goal.

Equipment: Four cones, two sets of coloured bibs, a supply of balls

Progressions: A competition to see which team scores the most goals. The coach can put a time-limit on each team to see how many goals they can achieve.

Drill 47

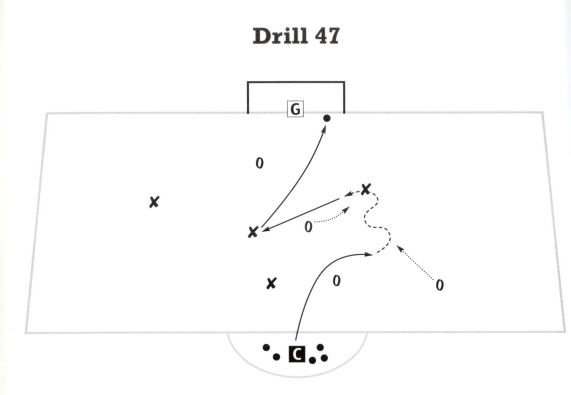

Purpose: Various shooting situations for snap-shots

Practice set-up: Two teams of three or four players must stay in the penalty area while the coach stands in the penalty arc with a good supply of balls. The coach serves the ball randomly into the penalty area for the nearest players to look for snap-shots. Alternatively, the players can pass or dribble before setting up their team-mates with a shot while the other team tries to prevent them from scoring. The coach serves the ball as soon as a shot is scored to keep the pressure on the players – just like a real match!

Equipment: A good supply of balls, two sets of coloured bibs

Progressions: The coach can add team scores to increase pressure or restrict play to one- or two-touch.

Drill 48

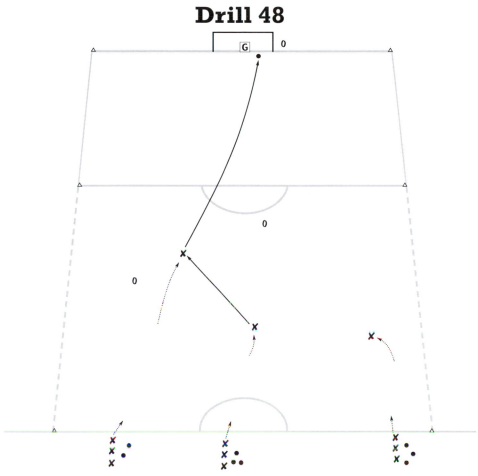

Purpose: Repeated shots and interpassing

Practice set-up: A channel is marked from the width of the penalty area down to the halfway line. Three files of players stand on the other side of the halfway line, but inside the channel, and face two defenders. Another defender acts as a ball-retriever. The first three players come out with the ball to play 3 vs 2 and try to score in the goal. As soon as the attack ends, the three attackers immediately move off to the sides of the field as the next 'wave of attack' emerges.

Equipment: Six cones, a good supply of balls

Progressions: The players work for a set time before rotating so that the defending file becomes the attacking file.

Drill 49

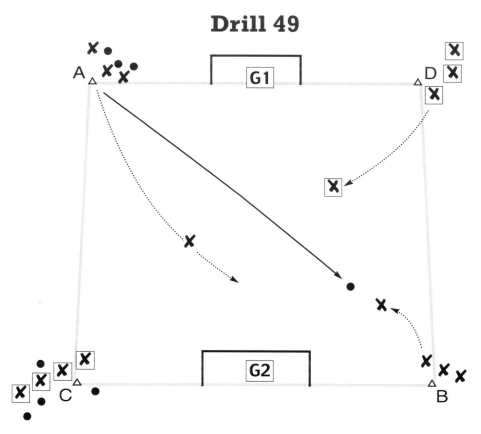

Purpose: To quickly exploit extra-man situation to get in shot at goal

Practice set-up: Four files of players (A, B, C, D) line up on the corners of a 20 yd square that has two portable goals and two goalkeepers. Files C and D play in the same colours; files A and C have a good supply of balls. The drill begins with player A passing diagonally to player B. Player A then runs in to support player B against the emerging defender player D to create a 2 vs 1 situation. A and B then try to score in goal 1. As soon as the action ends, players A and B join each other's files, while D joins C's file. The drill then continues from the opposite direction – player C passes diagonally to player D and they play 2 vs 1 with the emerging defender player B and try to score in goal 2.

Equipment: Four cones, two portable goals, a good supply of balls

Progressions: The teams can compete to see who scores the most goals

Drill 50

Purpose: Various shooting situations

Practice set-up: A channel is marked from the width of the penalty area to the halfway line. The coach, armed with a good supply of balls, stands in the centre circle, while two teams play 5 vs 5 in the channel. The coach serves a ball and the team that gains possession of the ball attacks. The attacking team is rewarded by getting the next service from the coach if they manage to get a shot at goal and the next two services if they actually score. The team defending can only get the next service if they can manage to get the ball from the attackers and get it to the coach on the halfway line. Whichever team gets most goals wins.

Equipment: Six cones, two sets of coloured bibs, a good supply of balls

Progressions: The coach can restrict play to two-touch to ensure plenty of shots.

Chapter 6

HEADING THE BALL

Heading the ball is a skill unique to soccer – no other sport uses the head to propel the ball. Although much of the game is played on the ground, heading is an integral part of soccer. Young players, no matter what their position, should be capable of dealing with the ball in the air, either in a defensive or attacking mode. However, heading is a skill which requires a logical and careful approach when introducing it to young footballers. Players at this stage should have experienced heading earlier in its basic form and should have built up a foundation of simple techniques. The aim of the following drills is to solidify and extend these technical skills so that the young player learns to become confident in heading the ball in more active and realistic situations.

Sol Campbell's tall and athletic physique cuts a dominating figure in the heart of England's defence. He is particularly effective when the ball is in the air and his sheer size and powerful spring enable him to power the ball away from the danger area. *Photo: Chris Lobina*

Drill 51

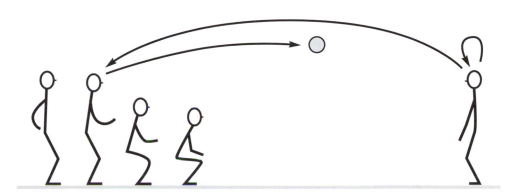

Purpose: Controlled heading of the ball

Practice set-up: A file of players faces a team-mate (the server) who stands 4–6 yds away with a ball. The server tosses the ball up and plays a controlled header to the first player in the file, who returns the ball with a header and quickly crouches down. After catching the returned header, the server heads the ball to the next player in line, who heads it back. The drill continues until the whole file have exchanged headers with the server. The server then changes places with another player until everyone has had a turn. The first file to complete a sequence of non-stop headers without the ball touching the ground wins.

Equipment: One ball

Progressions: The serving player stands further away to increase the difficulty.

Drill 52

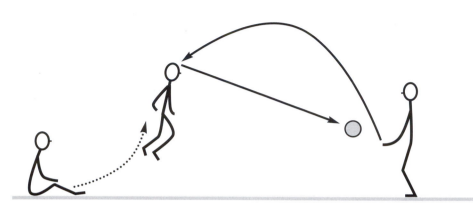

Purpose: To develop jumping ability and timing when heading the ball

Practice set-up: A player sits on the ground facing the coach or a player (the server), who has a ball in his hands, 5–8 yds away. The server shouts 'Up!' while tossing the ball in a high, looping service to the player. The player gets up quickly to jump and 'hang' in the air before heading the ball back to the server. He then sits down again quickly to await the next serve. The server gives the player 4–6 repeated services.

Equipment: One ball

Progressions: The server can add more repetitions.

Drill 53

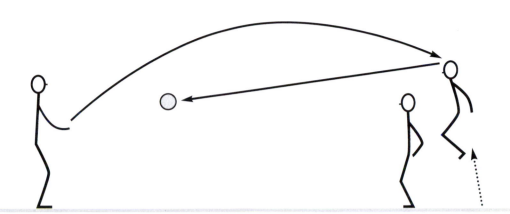

Purpose: Defensive heading against an opponent

Practice set-up: The player acting as the server stands with the ball 5–7 yds away from two other players, with one standing a yard behind the other. The back player receives a looped underarm service from the server, which goes over the first player's head. He jumps up and heads the ball back to the server over the first player's head. He receives six continuous services before the players change places. The first player does not move during the drill.

Equipment: One ball

Progressions: The server can toss the ball from further away or the non-heading player can provide some opposition with a little jump.

Drill 54

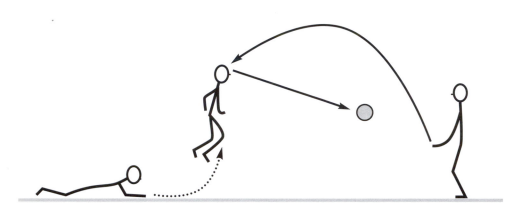

Purpose: Jumping ability and recovering to head the ball

Practice set-up: A player lies on the ground on his stomach facing the coach or a player (the server), who stands 5–8 yds away holding a ball. The server shouts 'Up!' and at the same time tosses the ball underarm in a high arc, giving the player time to rise. The player reacts quickly to the shout and service, and gets up to jump and head the ball back to the server. The drill continues for a set number of services.

Equipment: One ball

Progressions: Serve the ball from a little further away or add a few more repetitions.

Drill 55

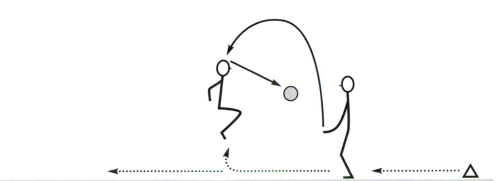

Purpose: Jumping to head the ball while moving backwards

Practice set-up: The players stand in pairs, one with the ball in his hands facing the other, who is 1-5 yds away. The player with the ball starts just in front of one cone and the players move towards another cone 20 yds away. While the server jogs forwards, feeding the ball high above the first player's head, the other player jogs backwards and jumps up to head the ball back for the server to catch at chest height. The server drives the other player backwards with continuous serves until the player reaches the other cone. After they reach the cone they reverse roles and move in the opposite direction, back towards the first cone.

Equipment: Two cones, one ball

Progressions: The server can drive the player in a backward, forward or sideways direction to vary the drill.

Drill 56

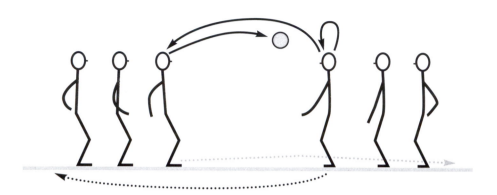

Purpose: Controlled heading while on the move

Practice set-up: Two files of players stand facing each other 1–6 yds apart. The first player in one file has the ball. He tosses it and heads it to the first player in the opposite file. He then moves in the direction of the ball, and joins the back of the opposite file. The players head the ball in sequence and count their highest score of continuous headers.

Equipment: One ball

Progressions: The players stand further apart to increase the difficulty of the exercise.

Drill 57

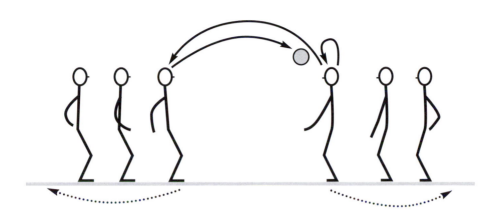

Purpose: Controlled heading while on the move

Practice set-up: Two files of players stand 1–6 yds apart and face each other. The first player in one file has the ball. The player with the ball tosses the ball up and heads it accurately to the first player on the other side, turning to run to the back of his own file as he does so. The player opposite heads the ball back and runs to the rear of his file. The drill continues with all players heading the ball in sequence. When the drill is completed the files count their highest score of continuous headers.

Equipment: One ball

Progressions: The players stand further apart to increase the difficulty of the exercise.

Drill 58

Purpose: Controlled heading

Practice set-up: Three players stand in a group 2–3 yds apart and proceed to keep the ball in the air by heading it to each other. Players are allowed no more than three consecutive headers before heading the ball to another player. Several groups of players compete and the group with the highest total of headers wins. Each player must remember to head the ball high in the air to give his team-mates a chance of heading the ball accurately each time.

Equipment: One ball

Progressions: The coach can call out a number from one to three. Each player in turn needs to keep the ball in the air by heading it for the designated number of times before heading it to the next player.

Drill 59

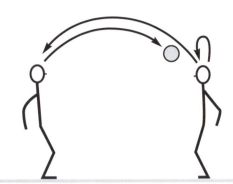

Purpose: Controlled heading

Practice set-up: Two players stand 2–3 yds apart and face each other. One player has a ball, which he serves to himself and heads to his partner so that they can keep it in the air. The drill then progresses with each player doing a little controlled 'bounce' header to himself before playing the second header to his partner. Later they can 'keep the ball up' on their own for longer sequences before returning it to their partner.

Equipment: One ball

Progressions: Each pair of players can compete to see which can produce the greatest number of consecutive headers. They start by heading the ball to each other in sequence (once, twice, three times etc.) to see how far they can go before losing control of the ball.

Drill 60

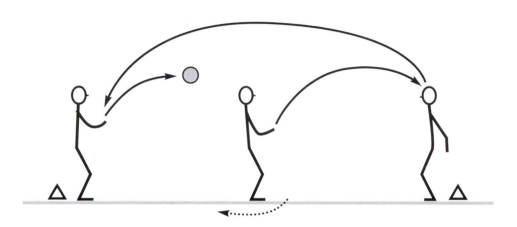

Purpose: Power heading

Practice set-up: Three players stand in a line, each one 2–6 yds apart from the next. The middle player holds the ball and feeds it underarm to one of the end players. The player who receives the ball heads it high and long over the middle player for the player at the other end to catch. The middle player turns to receive an underarm throw from this player and then he feeds the ball back to him so that he can head it long and high for the end player.

Equipment: Two cones, one ball

Progressions: Players move further apart so that the headers need to be longer. The players should change positions after ten repetitions.

Drill 61

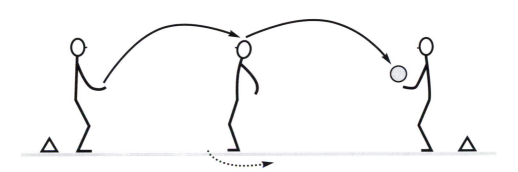

Purpose: Deflection heading in a backwards direction

Practice set-up: Three players stand in a line, each one 2-3 yds apart from the next. One of the end players holds the ball and feeds it underarm to the middle player so that he can deflect it backwards for the other end player to catch. The middle player wheels around to receive an underarm throw which he deflects backwards. The sequence continues from side to side for six to ten repetitions.

Equipment: Two cones, one ball

Progressions: The players stand a little further apart so the headers need to be longer, or instruct the end players to also head, rather than catch the ball so the drill is continuous.

Drill 62

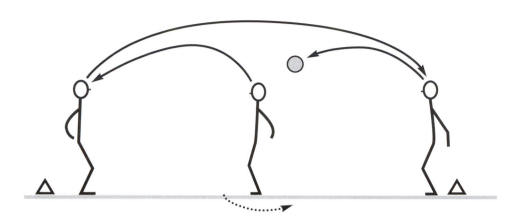

Purpose: Controlled power heading

Practice set-up: Three players stand in a line, each one 3 yds apart from the next. The middle player, who has a ball in his hands, faces one of the end players and proceeds to head the ball to him. This player immediately heads the ball over the middle player towards the other player at the end of the file. This player, in turn, heads the ball to the middle player, who has turned to face him. The middle player then heads the ball long and high to the other end player. The middle player keeps the sequence going by setting up the two end players with alternate short and long headers to complete the drill.

Equipment: Two cones, one ball

Progressions: The players stand a little further apart so the headers need to be longer.

Drill 63

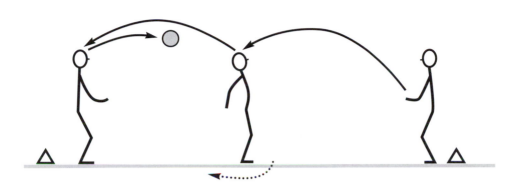

Purpose: Deflection and controlled heading

Practice set-up: Three players stand in a line, each one 2–3 yds apart from the next. One of the end players tosses the ball underarm to the middle player who is facing him. The middle player deflects the ball backwards to the other end player and turns quickly to receive a headed service. The middle player then heads the ball backwards to the first player. The three players look to keep a headed sequence going for as long as possible.

Equipment: Two cones, one ball

Progressions: Groups of players compete against each other to see who can keep the heading sequence going the longest.

Drill 64

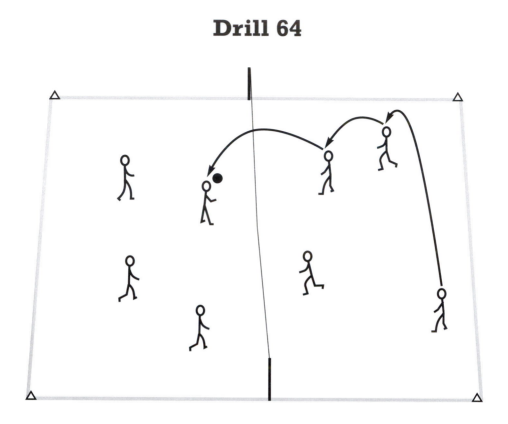

Purpose: Various heading techniques

Practice set-up: Two teams of four to five players play head-tennis on a court 15 yds square with a rope or net fastened above head height on the centre line. One player from a team serves by heading the ball over the net from the back line to start the game. At first, the players can allow the ball to bounce a few times on the ground but must use their feet to flick it up for a team-mate to head it back over the net. If the ball goes out of court or fails to go over the net, the team loses a point.

Equipment: Four cones, two poles, a net or rope, one ball

Progressions: Three players from each team must head the ball consecutively before returning it over the net.

Drill 65

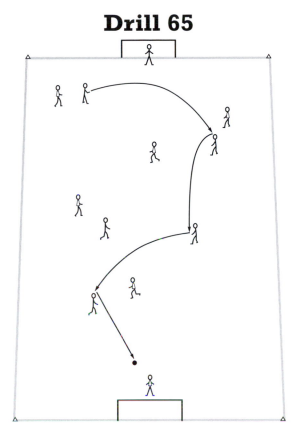

Purpose: Heading while under challenge

Practice set-up: Two teams of six players, including two goalkeepers in two portable goals, play in an area 40 yds long by 30 yds wide. The teams play throw-head-catch sequences, starting with a player throwing the ball high in the air to a team-mate, who heads it for another player to catch. Once a player catches the ball he cannot be obstructed as he tries to throw it. However, as soon as the ball is in the air all players are free to challenge for it. If a player throws the ball towards a team-mate and no-one heads it, possession goes to the other team. A goal can only be scored by a direct header during the throw-head-catch sequence.

Equipment: Four cones, two sets of coloured bibs, two portable goals, one ball

Progressions: The coach can allow the players to serve a controlled volley-kick from their hands each time instead of a throw.

Chapter 7

CROSSING AND FINISHING

Research has shown that at all levels of the game a high percentage of goals are scored from crosses from wide positions. Young players need to learn to cross the ball effectively from both sides of the field. Equally, they need to work out where and when they can make runs to get to the cross. Finally, they need to continuously practise the different techniques that are needed to convert the crosses into goals.

Youngsters, when learning to cross the ball, should start with a static ball first before moving on to a rolling ball, which is more difficult to direct. Finishing off crosses requires practice in timing a run to get to the ball and assessing the flight speed, angle and height of the incoming ball before deciding whether to head, volley, half-volley or hit it from the ground. The coach should start the drills with slower crosses and allow plenty of practice opportunities for the young players to develop their own techniques, as well as those taught by the coach, to finish off the cross with a strike at goal. It is a good idea to repeat the same type of cross for a set number of times so that the players get a lot of practice in one technique before they then learn a different technique to cope with a different situation.

All players in this age range, no matter what position they play, would do well to practise crossing and finishing so they can build these skills into their game play.

Opposite: **Thierry Henry, the French international wide player, took a little time to get going in the World Cup Finals in 1998, but when he eventually tuned in he devastated his opponents' defences. His blistering pace allowed him to get to the by-line regularly to deliver dangerous crosses, and to cut inside to shoot when least expected.** *Photo: Richard Martin*

Drill 66

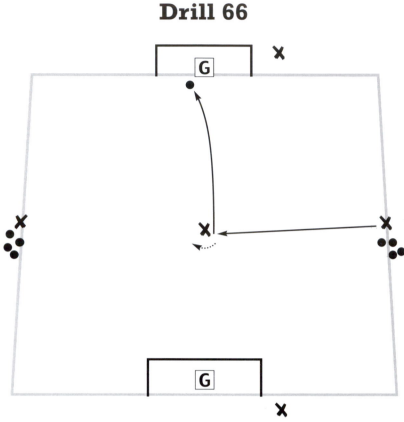

Purpose: Turning to finish from a centre cross

Practice set-up: A 20 yd square is marked out, with two portable goals defended by goalkeepers and one player behind each goal acting as a ball-retriever. Two players, each with a good supply of balls, stand at the halfway mark, facing a player who is positioned in the centre of the square. The players in the wide positions cross the ball for the central player to head or shoot at goal. The wide players cross the ball in sequence so the central player always receives a cross from one player to shoot at one goal before turning to receive a cross from the other player.

Equipment: Two portable goals, a good supply of balls

Progressions: The central player is given a set time before changing places with another player.

Drill 67

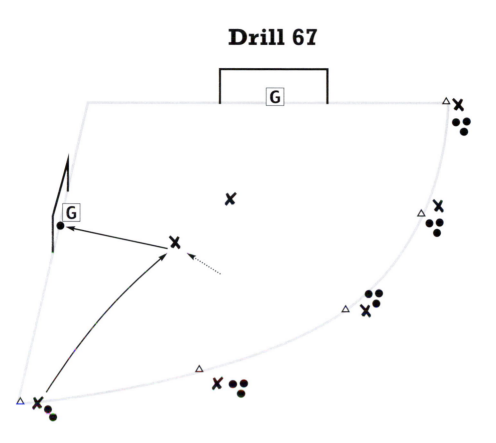

Purpose: Finishing from various crossing situations

Practice set-up: On the corner of a football field, two goals are erected 5–7 yds from the corner and on the outside lines. Two goalkeepers guard the goals and on an arc with a 20 yd radius, five players, who act as servers, spread themselves evenly with three to five balls each. Two strikers stand in the centre of the area, 10 yds from the goals. The drill begins with the server on one of the corners crossing the ball into the area where the two strikers look to finish with headers or shots. Each striker has their own goal and the servers serve in sequence until all the balls are used up. At this point two more strikers take over.

Equipment: Two portable goals, five cones, a good supply of balls

Progressions: The two strikers shooting at goal can have various conditions imposed on them, such as first-time shots only allowed, or each striker can score in *either* goal.

Drill 68

Purpose: Timing runs to finish from crosses that are hit on the run by a wide player

Practice set-up: On a football field, a channel is marked out from the touchline, along the penalty area, and up to the halfway line. A portable goal is placed on the penalty area and opposite the field goal. Each goal is defended by a goalkeeper. Two files of players each with a supply of balls face each other at opposite ends of the channel. The first player runs with the ball along the channel towards the opposite side and crosses the ball for the two strikers, who try to score. As soon as the first player hits the cross, the first player at the other end runs past him with the ball at his feet along the channel to hit a cross to the strikers. The first player who hits a cross must recover quickly and turn to chase the player running up the channel to put him under pressure, but without actually tackling him. Each player goes through the same sequence of running with the ball as they are chased and then chasing the next player.

Equipment: Five cones, a good supply of balls, a portable goal

Progressions: Move the channel to the opposite flank so the players can practise with the other foot.

Drill 69

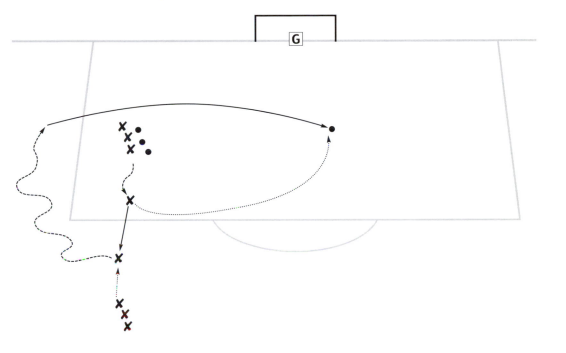

Purpose: Co-ordinating running with the ball and crossing

Practice set-up: Towards the side of the penalty area, two files of players face each other 8–12 yds apart. Each player from the file nearest to the goal has a ball. The first player dribbles forwards slowly as the first player from the opposite file approaches at about the same speed. The player with the ball gives a short pass and moves in a big horseshoe-shaped run towards the front of the goal. The receiving player takes the ball and runs wide with it before hitting a cross to the first player, who finishes with a shot or header. Both players retire to opposite files as the next two players continue the drill sequence.

Equipment: A good supply of balls

Progressions: Quicken the practice tempo or ask players to concentrate on a particular move (e.g. far post cross and header). Both players need to synchronise their movements with each other to allow effective strikes at goal.

Drill 70

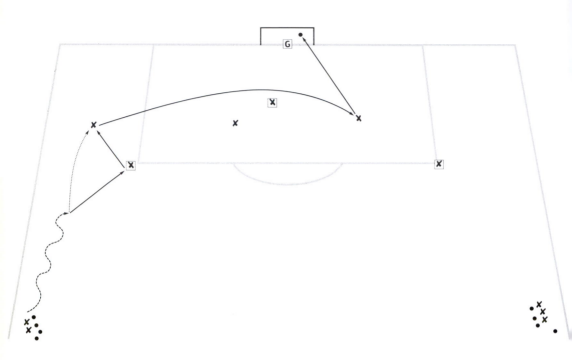

Purpose: Finishing from crosses while under challenge

Practice set-up: Two files of players line up on the flanks of a football field, 15 yds away from two players positioned at the corners of the penalty area. Two attackers and one defender are positioned in and cannot leave the penalty area. The wide players, who have a ball each, come forwards alternately and play a wall-pass with the corner players before hitting a cross for the attackers to try and score as the defender tries to prevent them from scoring.

Equipment: One to three coloured bibs, a good supply of balls

Progressions: Add another defender to the penalty area.

Drill 71

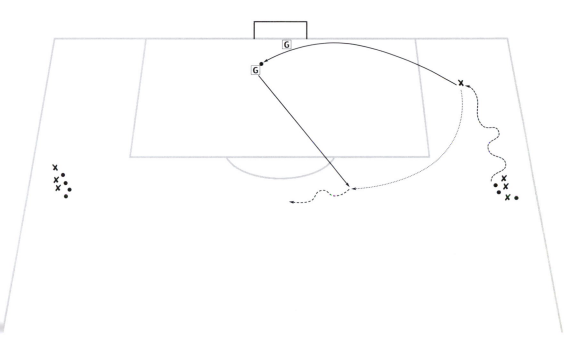

Purpose: General crossing

Practice set-up: Two files of players stand in wide positions on a football field. They each have a good supply of balls and face the goal, which is guarded by two goalkeepers. The first player in one file runs up the flank with the ball before crossing the ball into the penalty area, where the nearest goalkeeper saves and holds it. The player then turns and runs around the penalty area, and the goalkeeper rolls the ball back to him. The player dribbles the ball to the other side so the first player from the other file can continue the drill.

Equipment: A good supply of balls

Progressions: The coach can ask the players to take the ball wider, or run more quickly with it, before crossing.

Drill 72

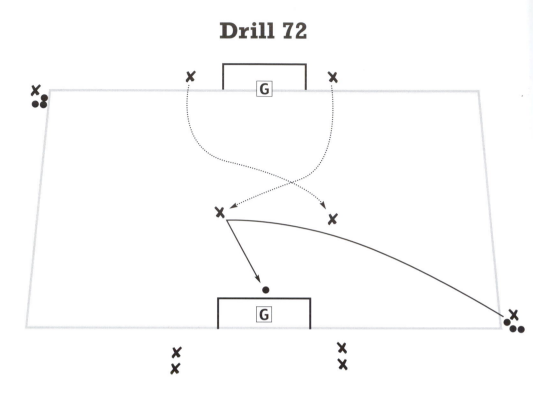

Purpose: Timing runs and crosses

Practice set-up: In an area measuring 15–20 yds long by 30 yds wide with two portable goals guarded by two goalkeepers, two players stand in opposite corners, each with a good supply of balls. Files of players line up at the sides of the goals and the first two players from one end start with a 'cross-run' towards the opposite goal. They time their approach to meet a cross coming in from one of the corner players, and attempt to finish with a shot or header. They then join the back of the opposite file as the first two players from the opposite end set off to attack the other goal.

Equipment: Two portable goals, a good supply of balls

Progressions: Create a competition in which players get two points for a headed goal and one point for a shot.

Drill 73

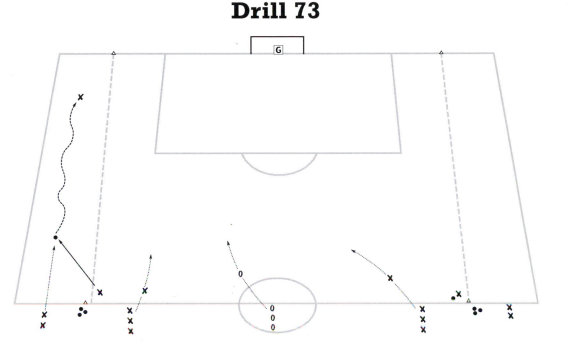

Purpose: Finishing and crossing in a realistic game situation

Practice set-up: On a football field, channels are marked on each flank from the goal line to the halfway line. A file of players stands in each channel at the halfway line. Two servers are positioned, each with a good supply of balls, 6-10 yds from the players in the channels and along the halfway line. Three files of players are positioned a few yards apart in between the channels and along the halfway line. The middle file of players are defenders; the other two files are attackers. The drill begins with one of the servers passing the ball to the first player in the nearest channel file (the winger) who runs with the ball in the channel. This is a signal for the first two attackers and defender to emerge from their files to attack the cross from the winger. The defender looks to intercept the ball while the two attackers go on various runs to make space so they can finish effectively. The practice continues from the opposite side.

Equipment: Four cones, two portable goals, a good supply of balls

Progressions: After a set time change the attackers and wingers so all the players get finishing and crossing practice.

Drill 74

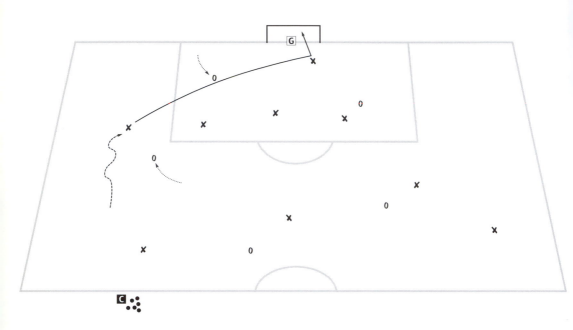

Purpose: Finishing and crossing in a realistic game situation

Practice set-up: On a football field five attackers and three defenders play possession football in one half of the field, but they are *not* allowed to enter the penalty area. Inside the penalty area four attackers play against two defenders. These six players *cannot* leave the penalty area. The coach, who has a good supply of balls, starts the drill from the halfway line. The attackers outside the penalty area try to move up the flanks and cross for one of the attackers in the penalty area to try and score with a header or shot. After a strike the coach restarts the drill.

Equipment: Two sets of coloured bibs, a good supply of balls

Progressions: The coach can add an extra defender inside or outside the penalty area.

Drill 75

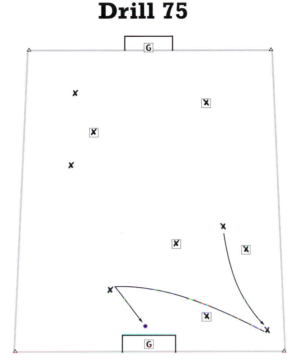

Purpose: Heading under challenge from high, wide, and lobbed centres

Practice set-up: Two teams, each with a goalkeeper, play in a marked area measuring 40 yds long by 30 yds wide. The players play a sequence of 'volley-head-catch', where both teams try to score in the opposition's goal with a header. The drill starts with one player holding the ball and gently tossing it up in a controlled way, before using his foot to volley the ball high in the air towards a team-mate. The receiving player tries to head it to another team-mate while under challenge from an opponent. The player who then catches the ball cannot be challenged. However, as soon as the ball is volleyed, players from both teams look to jump and head the ball to their team-mates. The coach needs to ensure that players challenge in a safe manner.

Equipment: Two sets of coloured bibs, a good supply of balls, two portable goals, four cones

Progressions: Instead of always catching the ball from a header, the coach can permit the players to head the ball two or three times consecutively if it is in the air and 'headable'.

Chapter 8

GOALKEEPING

The goalkeeper is the only specialist in the team so he needs to develop his own specific technical skills and individual tactics for the position. The modern keeper's role has widened considerably in the last few years. New legislation, such as the back-pass rule, has forced goalkeepers to improve their kicking and passing techniques. Technology has advanced with the advent of footballs that can move faster and deviate more in flight. Tactical developments mean that the keeper needs to 'read the game' and direct his defence as well as distributing the ball well by throwing or kicking to set up effective attacks for his team. All of these changes have increased the demands on the goalkeeper.

The drills contained in this chapter will help young goalkeepers to build the necessary technical skills, knowledge and tactical acumen to play in the position with authority and confidence.

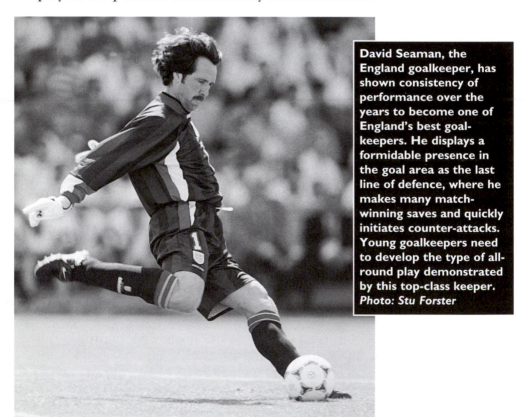

David Seaman, the England goalkeeper, has shown consistency of performance over the years to become one of England's best goalkeepers. He displays a formidable presence in the goal area as the last line of defence, where he makes many match-winning saves and quickly initiates counter-attacks. Young goalkeepers need to develop the type of all-round play demonstrated by this top-class keeper.
Photo: Stu Forster

Drill 76

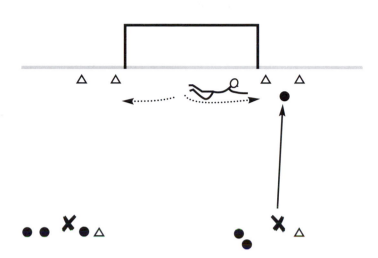

Purpose: Diving low to deflect the ball from goal

Practice set-up: On soft grass or sand, mark two small goals 2 yds wide with cones just in front of and on each side of a portable goal. Two players with three balls each stand facing the small goals at two cones placed 1–2 yds away. The goalkeeper starts in the centre of the two goals. Each player alternately passes the ball slowly along the ground, aiming to put it through his goal. The goalkeeper slides or dives along the surface and looks to deflect the ball, getting up quickly to recover and deflect the ball on the other side. How many consecutive saves can the goalkeeper make?

Equipment: Six cones, a portable goal, a good supply of balls

Progressions: Speed up the practice as the goalkeeper improves his technique.

Drill 77

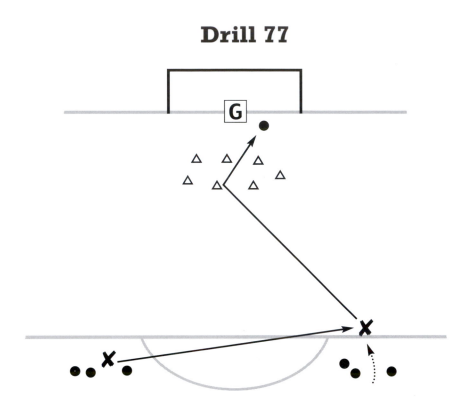

Purpose: Quicken reactions and shot-stopping

Practice set-up: The goalkeeper defends his goal with a number of cones that are placed in front of the goal area. Two players positioned each side of the penalty arc interpass and shoot, looking for deflections from the cones as the goalkeeper uses his reflexes to deflect the shots. As soon as the goalkeeper saves the ball another shot is fired at goal to maintain the flow.

Equipment: Six to eight cones, a good supply of balls

Progressions: Speed up the shots at goal. The goalkeeper should go for every shot.

Drill 78

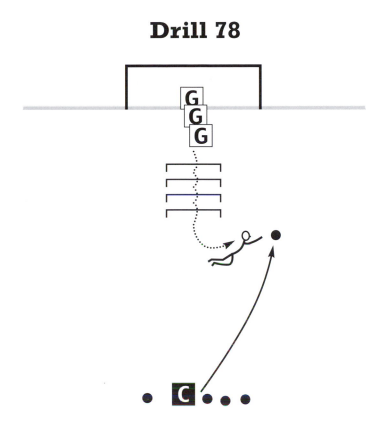

Purpose: Diving technique and general agility

Practice set-up: A file of goalkeepers stand in the goal area facing a row of small hurdles 6–12 inches high. The coach stands on the other side of the hurdles, with a supply of balls. Each goalkeeper runs quickly over the hurdles and receives a ball that is tossed to the side by the coach. They must dive, hold the ball, return it quickly and move to the back of the file to await their next turn.

Equipment: Six hurdles, a few balls

Progressions: The coach can serve the ball a little wider or higher as the drill continues, to make the exercise more difficult for the goalkeeper as he dives for the ball.

Drill 79

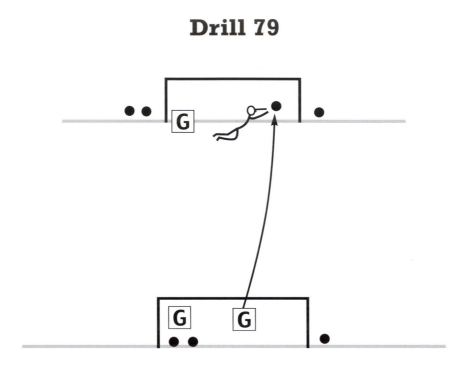

Purpose: Shot-stopping and distribution of the ball

Practice set-up: Two pairs of goalkeepers defend two portable goals. Each pair has a supply of balls. One goalkeeper tries to score in the opposite goal while the two goalkeepers in that goal try to save his shot. The receiving goalkeepers then throw or kick the ball back. All four goalkeepers try alternately to score or save the ball, ensuring that they keep the pressure on each other.

Equipment: Two portable goals, a good supply of balls

Progressions: Move the goals closer together. Alternatively, the ball may be hit or thrown with greater force (while still maintaining accuracy) to create opportunities for better saves.

Drill 80

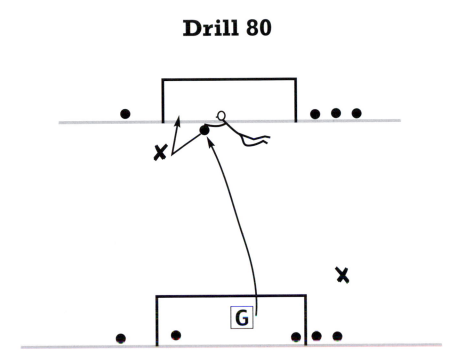

Purpose: To stop shots and keep the ball safe

Practice set-up: Two goalkeepers defend two portable goals and each has a good supply of balls. The goalkeepers take turns to roll the ball along the ground and shoot at the opposite goal. The other goalkeeper looks to save the ball. A player is positioned a few yards from the side of each goal and can score from any shots that rebound from the goalkeeper or that the goalkeeper fails to hold.

Equipment: Two portable goals, a good supply of balls

Progressions: The shots can be struck harder so it is more difficult for the goalkeeper to hold on to them or to deflect them to safer areas.

Drill 81

Purpose: Correct diving technique

Practice set-up: The goalkeepers form a file a yard to the side of a ball, which is placed on the ground. The first goalkeeper faces the coach, who has a ball in his hands and stands 3 yds away. The coach tosses the ball a foot off the ground to the far side of the ball on the ground. The goalkeeper dives to deflect or catch the ball in the air, ensuring that he goes directly over the ball on the ground without touching it.

Equipment: A good supply of balls

Progressions: Gradually toss the ball higher so that the drill becomes more difficult.

Drill 82

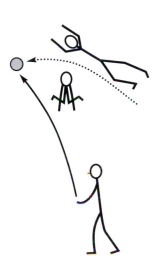

Purpose: Diving to save high shots

Practice set-up: The goalkeepers form a file a yard to the side of a player who crouches on the ground. The coach, who has a ball in his hands, stands 3 yds in front of the crouching player. The coach serves the ball off the ground and to the side for the first goalkeeper to dive and deflect or catch. The goalkeeper should dive on both sides, taking care not to touch or make contact with the crouching player. The goalkeeper should push off so that both feet are off the ground as he dives.

Equipment: A good supply of balls

Progressions: Serve the ball higher or wider to increase the difficulty for the goalkeeper.

Drill 83

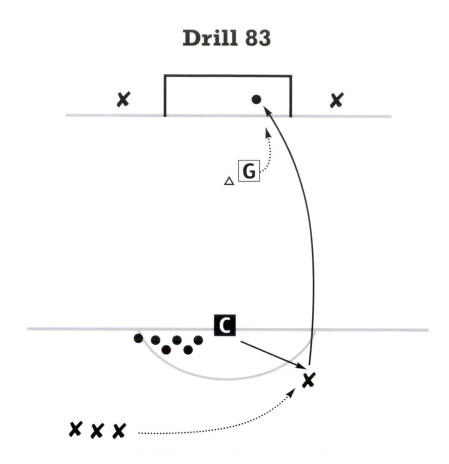

Purpose: Dealing with an overhead chip shot

Practice set-up: The goalkeeper starts in the centre of the goal area, facing the coach, who stands in the penalty arc, and a file of players, who stand 12–16 yds away. The coach, who has a supply of balls, rolls them gently to each player in turn. The players try to chip the ball over the goalkeeper to score. The goalkeeper can't go after the ball until it is kicked and he must return to the same position before each shot. Good footwork is required from the goalkeeper as he runs after the ball before attempting to 'flip' it over the cross-bar.

Equipment: A good supply of balls, one cone

Progressions: Each goalkeeper works for a set time and compares his score with the other goalkeepers.

Drill 84

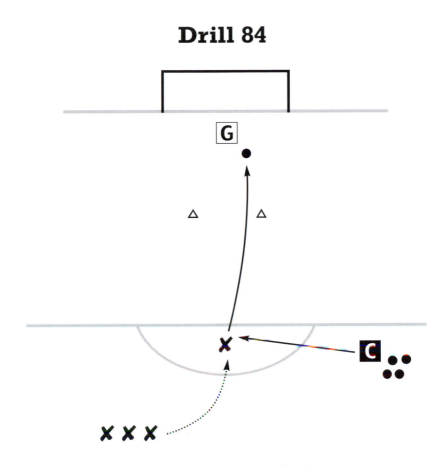

Purpose: Dealing with hard shots close to the body

Practice set-up: The goalkeeper stands just in front of the goal line. Two cones 3 yds apart are placed halfway between the goal and the penalty arc. The coach, who has a supply of balls, stands to one side of the penalty arc, and a file of players stands further back and behind the penalty arc. The coach plays a gentle pass to each player in turn and they shoot between the cones. The goalkeeper tries to save the ball. Only shots that go through the cones count, so the players need to be accurate to give the goalkeeper worthwhile practice.

Equipment: Two cones, a good supply of balls

Progressions: As the goalkeeper improves, move the players a little closer to the goal so that the shots are harder. Ensure the goalkeepers wear gloves.

Drill 85

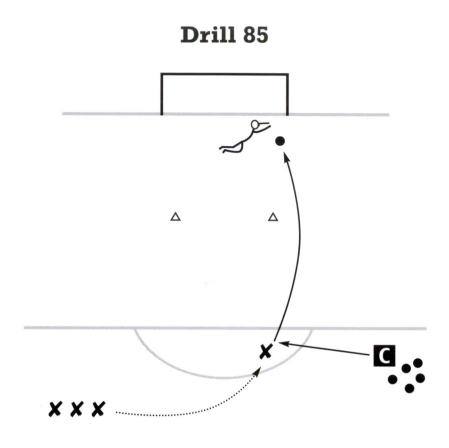

Purpose: To practise dealing with shots that go wide to the corners

Practice set-up: The goalkeeper stands just in front of the goal line. Two cones positioned 5 yds apart are placed halfway between the goal and penalty arc. The coach, who has a supply of balls, stands to one side of the penalty arc, and a file of players stands further back and behind the penalty arc. The coach plays a short pass for each player to shoot outside the cones. The goalkeeper tries to save each shot.

Equipment: Two cones, a good supply of balls

Progressions: Change the goalkeepers after a set time and ask the players to keep varying their shots to keep the goalkeeper guessing and to test him.

Chapter 9

TURNING AND SCREENING THE BALL

Most players are reasonably sound when playing forwards and facing their opponent's goal, but not so good when playing with their backs towards the same goal. This is because their vision is restricted and movement is more awkward when moving backwards than forwards. To play the game well all players have to learn to do this, particularly the front players, and to a lesser extent the midfield players, who will receive many passes on the ground and in the air with their back to the goal. In these circumstances, young players must learn to screen the ball, hold it against challenging opponents and 'lay off' accurate passes to team-mates who have arrived to support them. They must also see the opportunities to suddenly surprise the close-marking defender and turn past him with the ball to get into a more advantageous position. The drills in this chapter will help young players become more adept at playing with their back to goal and in the process they will become better all-round players.

Jamie Redknapp, the England midfielder, is beginning to fulfil his early potential now that he has developed his all-round play. When receiving the ball with his back to goal and opponents breathing down his neck he can turn away with the ball or hold it up until help arrives. *Photo: Shaun Botterill*

111

Drill 86

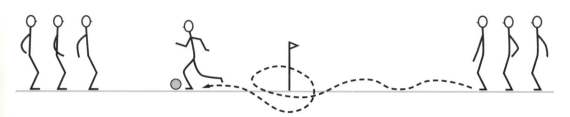

Purpose: Turning with the ball while on the run

Practice set-up: Two files of players face each other 12–15 yds apart, with a flag pole placed in the centre. The first player in one file, who has a ball at his feet, dribbles it towards the pole and proceeds around the pole before dribbling the ball to the next player on the opposite side. The drill is repeated in the opposite direction.

Equipment: One flag pole, one ball

Progressions: Players should use both feet and various parts of them when turning with the ball.

Drill 87

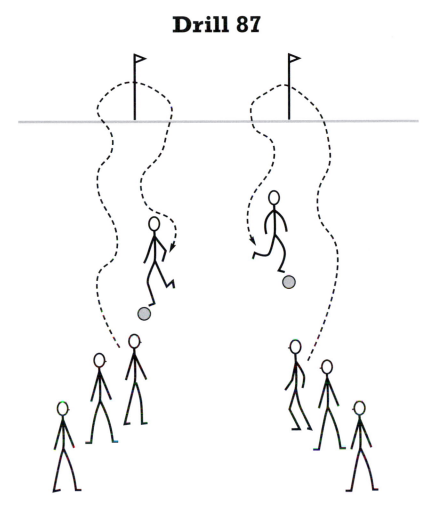

Purpose: Turning quickly with the ball while on the run

Practice set-up: Two files of players stand slightly to the side of each other, each facing a pole in the ground 10–15 yds away. The first player in each file has a ball at his feet and both players dribble the ball simultaneously until they reach their pole. Then they quickly dribble and turn with the ball around their pole and take the ball back to their file for the next player to repeat the drill.

Equipment: Two flag poles, two balls per file

Progressions: The drill can be set up as a competition where each player must repeat the drill a set number of times or be timed.

Drill 88

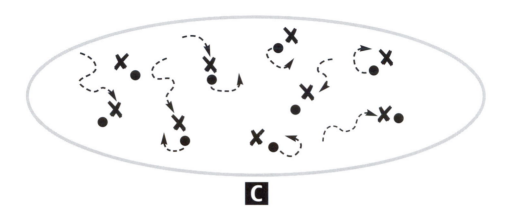

C

Purpose: Various turns with the ball

Practice set-up: A number of players, each with a ball, dribble inside a circle that is 10 yds in diameter (same size as the centre circle) so that it is quite congested. The coach calls 'turn' or whistles, to signal that the players need to execute a quick turn with the ball before dribbling on and awaiting the next whistle.

Equipment: A good supply of balls

Progressions: The players should be shown various turns and dummies that they have to practise on the coach's command.

Drill 89

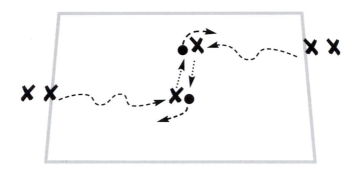

Purpose: Dribbling and turning with the ball

Practice set-up: Two files of players stand slightly to the side of each other and 10-12 yds apart. The first player in each file has a ball at his feet and proceeds to run with it in a straight direction until the halfway mark when he is opposite the other player. He stops the ball with his foot, leaves his ball and steps across to take the other player's ball – as the other player takes *his* ball. He turns with the ball and dribbles it to the next player in his file, who repeats the sequence.

Equipment: Two balls

Progressions: Speed up play, and turn with the ball in different ways.

Drill 90

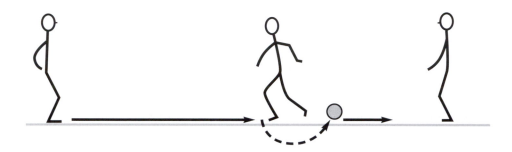

Purpose: Turning quickly with the ball

Practice set-up: Players in groups of three stand in line 3–4 yds apart. One of the end players who has a ball passes it to the middle player, who takes no more than three touches to turn with the ball under his control and pass to the other end player. The player receiving the ball now passes to the middle player, who turns again with the ball and passes it to the first end player. After a set number of passes or set time, the players change around.

Equipment: One ball

Progressions: The middle player is only allowed two touches or must vary his technique with each pass that he receives.

Drill 91

Purpose: Quick turning with the ball

Practice set-up: The players assemble in groups of four and stand in a line. Two middle players stand back-to-back, facing the two outside players who stand 3-4 yds away and have a ball each. The two outside players pass the ball simultaneously to the two middle players. The two middle players turn with the ball and pass it to the other outside player. The process is repeated in the opposite direction. Both players turning with the ball should use the same foot and turn in the same direction or to the same side to avoid a collision.

Equipment: Two balls

Progressions: Change the players after a set time, speed up play and vary the turning techniques.

Drill 92

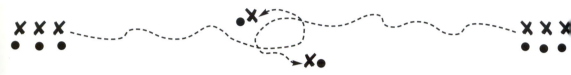

Purpose: Turning under semi-active challenge

Practice set-up: Two files of players face each other 10–12 yds apart. Each player has a ball. The first two players from each file dribble the ball towards each other. When they reach each other, about halfway between the two files, they turn around each other with the ball, and then continue to the opposite files where the next two players continue the drill. The players should always remember to use the *same* foot and move the *same* side with the ball.

Equipment: A ball for each player

Progressions: The players should practise with both feet and use various techniques.

Drill 93

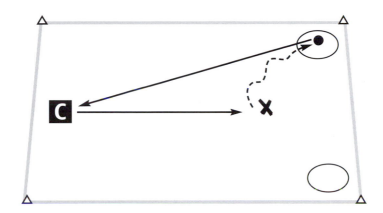

Purpose: Various turns with the ball

Practice set-up: A small channel measuring 15 yds long by 8 yds wide is marked on the ground. Two small circles are marked in two corners behind a player who stands facing the coach, who has a ball at his feet. The coach proceeds to pass the ball directly to the player calling 'left' or 'right' as he does. The player quickly turns to try and place the ball in the circle on the appropriate side. He then passes the ball back to the coach and awaits the next service. The players should practise using both feet.

Equipment: One ball, four cones, two circles marked on the ground

Progressions: Later a defender can be added who stands between the player and the circles.

Drill 94

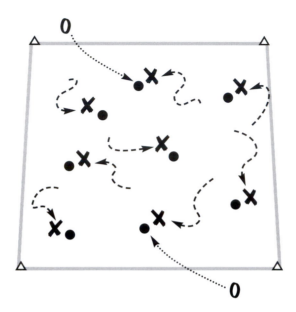

Purpose: Screening and turning with the ball while under challenge

Practice set-up: A group of players, who each have a ball, dribbles inside a 10 yd square while two players acting as defenders stand outside the area. The drill begins with both defenders challenging any of the dribblers inside the square. The dribblers screen or turn with the ball to evade their opponents. If a defender wins the ball he keeps it; the person who lost it becomes the defender and goes looking to challenge any other player to get a ball for himself.

Equipment: Four cones, a good supply of balls

Progressions: Add more defenders. Make sure defenders tackle correctly and don't foul the players screening the ball.

Drill 95

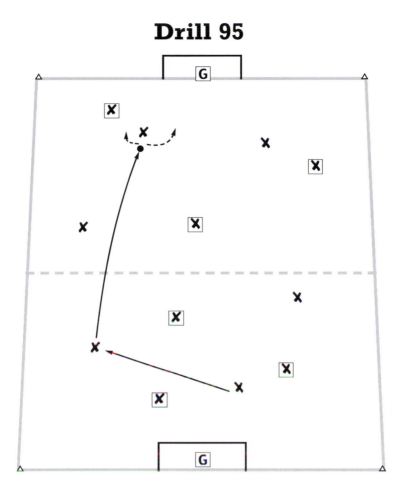

Purpose: Turning and screening the ball in realistic game situations

Practice set-up: On a field measuring 30 yds long by 25 yds wide with a halfway line and two portable goals defended by goalkeepers. Two teams of six players position three players in their defending half and three players in their attacking half. The players must remain in their designated half and play 3 vs 3. Goals can only be scored from the attacking half, which will encourage players to turn or screen the ball.

Equipment: Four cones, two portable goals, two sets of coloured bibs, one ball

Progressions: Add an extra defender to each team to encourage turning and screening the ball.

Chapter 10

WARMING DOWN

It is very important that young players enjoy their football. To this end, the coach should always strive to finish the practice session with activities that satisfy two needs in the youngsters. First, the work at the end of the practice should be somewhat lighter physically and mentally to allow the body and mind to gradually return to its normal state. The coach needs to help youngsters appreciate the need for warming down so that the body can recover more fully from waste products in the muscles caused by the physical exertion. Second, this work should also be a fun

activity where players can perform less intensively and more light-heartedly together. This is a good way to end each session because it will aid teamwork, friendships and promote team spirit in youngsters who love the fun element at this stage. Play down the winning with any competitions here. Let the players enjoy the exercise and warm down gradually so that it begins to become a habit – a good one for a young player to acquire!

Juan Veron, the Argentinian midfielder, is a tireless runner – a 'Mr Perpetual Motion'. His extraordinary fitness allows him to move all over the field for the entire match. A player's physical condition is built up on the training field with the correct preparation and fitness-based activities, including a thorough warm-up and warm-down. *Photo: Claudio Villa*

Drill 96

Purpose: General light running and enjoyment, encouragement of team spirit

Practice set-up: Files of 5–8 players stand facing a cone 15–20 yds away. The first player, who has a ball in his arms, runs around the cone and back to his team again. He turns his back to them and passes it overhead to the next player, who takes the ball from him and passes the ball through his legs to the next player, who passes the ball overhead. The sequence of over-and-under continues through the file until the ball reaches the end player. The end player runs around the cone and starts the sequence again. The drill continues until each file has finished a set number of sequences.

Equipment: One cone, one ball

Progressions: Players can dribble the ball rather than run with it in their arms.

Drill 97

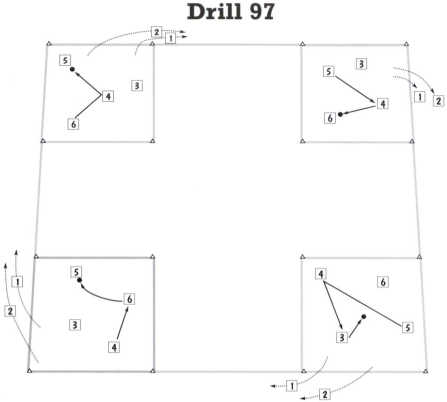

Purpose: Passing, movement and recovery

Practice set-up: In a 40 yd square, four smaller 12 yd squares are marked and 6–10 players stand in each. There is one ball for each square lying on the ground and the players are paired off (e.g. 1 and 2, 3 and 4, etc.). The drill starts with all the players passing and moving in their squares for a set time until the coach blows his whistle. This is the signal for the first pair of players from each square to jog together all the way around the outside of the area without the ball as the remaining players continue passing and moving off the ball. As soon as the jogging pairs arrive back at their respective squares, they join in the passing and moving and the next pair (i.e. 3 and 4) set off running around the area until all the pairs have each achieved at least one circuit.

Equipment: Four balls, sixteen cones, four sets of coloured bibs

Progressions: Players can perform set stretching exercises on their way around the rectangle.

Drill 98

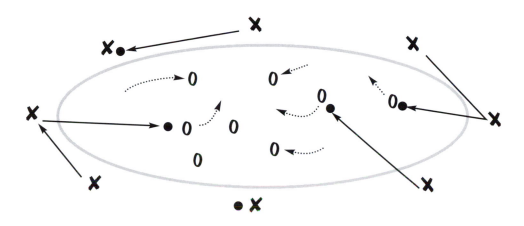

Purpose: Target hitting and general agility

Practice set-up: Two teams of 6–8 players are assembled. One team stands in the centre circle (or indoor hall) and the other team is positioned outside with a supply of balls. The outside players, the 'kickers', can pass to each other and try to drive the ball *below* waist height so that it hits one of the inside players, the 'dodgers'. If it does, the player is out and leaves the circle. The coach times how long it takes to get the whole team out. Both teams cannot go inside or outside the circle, depending on their roles, i.e. kickers cannot go inside; dodgers cannot go outside.

Equipment: A good supply of balls

Progressions: The teams change over and try to beat their previous score by hitting players more quickly.

Drill 99

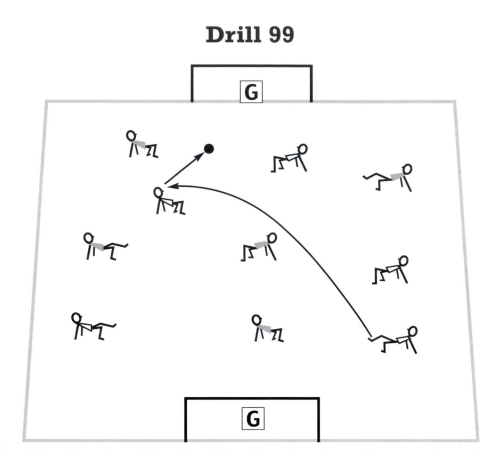

Purpose: Agility and enjoyment

Practice set-up: On an area measuring 20 yds by 15 yds with two portable goals, two teams play 'crab' football. All players must move along the ground without getting up to kneel or stand. They can dribble the ball, pass, head and shoot. However, only the goalkeepers can use their hands. (This drill can also be done indoors.)

Equipment: Two portable goals, two sets of coloured bibs, one soft ball

Progressions: The two goalkeepers can only kneel to defend their goal.

Drill 100

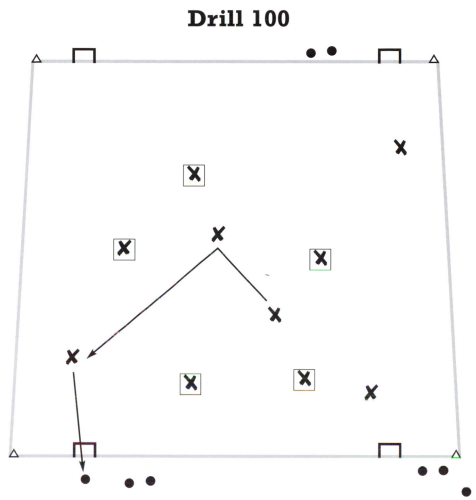

Purpose: Switch play

Practice set-up: In a 25 yd square, four small goals (about 1 yd wide by 2 ft high) are placed at the corners. Two teams play football as normal, except that they can score in the two far goals and must defend their own two goals. There are no goalkeepers and a point is awarded for each goal scored.

Equipment: Four goals, four cones, two sets of coloured bibs, a few balls

Progressions: Another ball can be introduced so that the players use two balls.

Drill 101

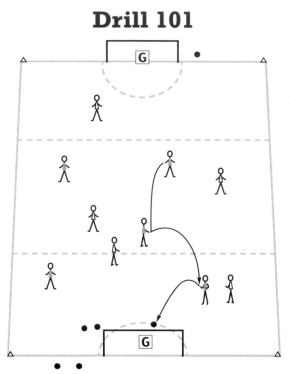

Purpose: General team fun, light action and handling skills

Practice set-up: An area 25 yds long by 20 yds wide is set up, with two goals defended by goalkeepers who are not allowed to come out of a semi-circle of 5 yds in diameter, which is marked in front of the goal. Two shooting zones are marked at both ends of the field, 8–10 yds from the goal lines. Two teams play modified handball in which they pass the ball to each other by hand, ensuring that they don't move or take a step when they have possession of the ball – they can move wherever they like when they do not have the ball. To score, they throw the ball into the goal with the goalkeeper attempting to save it. However, they must be in the shooting zone before they can shoot. If players drop a pass, or the intended pass hits the ground, or a defender intercepts a pass (without tackling for the ball), the opposing team gains possession of the ball.

Equipment: Four cones, two portable goals, two sets of coloured bibs, a few balls

Progressions: Introduce a rule that the players must pass within 2 or 3 seconds, otherwise possession goes to the other team.